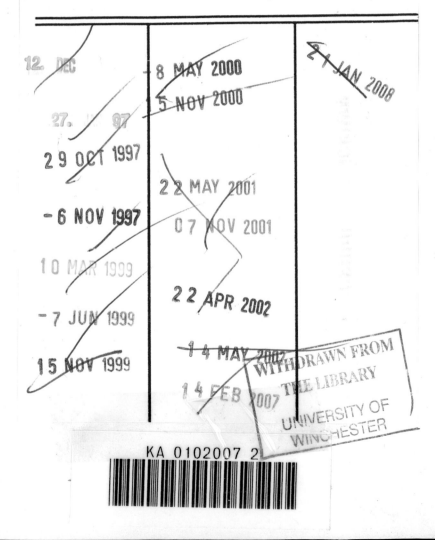

A GUIDE TO THE NATIONAL CURRICULUM

A Guide to the
National Curriculum

Bob Moon

Oxford University Press

1991

Oxford University Press, Walton Street, Oxford OX2 6DP

Oxford   New York   Toronto
Delhi   Bombay   Calcutta   Madras   Karachi
Kuala Lumpur   Singapore   Hong Kong   Tokyo
Nairobi   Dar es Salaam   Cape Town
Melbourne   Auckland

and associated companies in
Berlin   Ibadan

Oxford is a trade mark of Oxford University Press

ISBN 0 19 919073 9 (hardback)
ISBN 0 19 919075 5 (paperback)

Printed in Great Britain

A wide range of people have contributed to the information and ideas within this guide. Officers from the national councils (such as the National Curriculum Council) have provided informal advice on points of detail and the likely direction of policy in the future. Local Education Authority advisory staff have been helpful at numerous conferences up and down the country. Keith Hedger and Mike Raleigh of Shropshire provided a useful detailed commentary on the guide. My colleagues Janet Maybin, Patricia Murphy, Christine Shiu and Will Swann looked at specific sections. Sheila Walters patiently produced the manuscript. Rob Scriven, Caroline Mardall and Helen Giltrow provided all the necessary publisher's support. Finally, I would like to thank Barbara Vander, who first suggested that a guide such as this would be of interest and value.

Bob Moon

Contents

Introduction

The National Curriculum represents one of the most significant educational reforms of this century. It will have a major influence on schooling and on the work of teachers, governors, parents and employers. The school experience of future generations of young people is being transformed.

This guide outlines the structure of the National Curriculum, the way it is being introduced through the 1990s, and the form that school and national tests and assessment will take. The aim is to provide a straightforward, explanatory account of the central characteristics of the National Curriculum, including the technical terms and procedures used in schools. The guide also attempts to provide an insight into how the National Curriculum is working, looking at appropriate extracts from the extensive range of publications used by teachers in schools.

The introduction of a National Curriculum created considerable controversy. Political and academic debates still surround many aspects of the plans. One section of the guide sets out some of the problems, and the list of further reading includes a number of books that explore these in further detail.

In using this guide, two important points need to be borne in mind. Firstly it does not attempt to serve as a substitute for the statutory orders, official regulations and other formal documentation associated with the National Curriculum. Some of this formal documentation is daunting, even for the interested reader, but it does prescribe the legal basis upon which the National Curriculum is established. Three national councils exist to support and monitor the National Curriculum: the National Curriculum Council (NCC), the Curriculum Council for Wales (CCW) and the Schools Examinations and Assessment Council (SEAC). All produce a variety of publications, as does the Department of Education and Science and Her Majesty's Stationery Office. These should be referred to for any legal interpretations. Secondly it should be stressed that the information and ideas set out in the guide are best supplemented by contact and involvement with schools. No two schools are alike, and the

x

way the National Curriculum is taught will vary from school to school. However, a central core of curriculum opportunities and entitlements for all children is now enshrined in law. This guide is a contribution towards ensuring that this is appreciated and understood by everyone with an interest and involvement in education.

Bob Moon
Oxford, October 1990

SECTION 1

What is the National Curriculum?

In order to understand the National Curriculum, you first need to become familiar with a small number of terms and phrases. These, however, are straightforward not only for teachers, governors and parents but also, perhaps with the exception of the very youngest, for pupils in schools.

The National Curriculum forms an important part of the Education Reform Act that became law in the summer of 1988. The aims of the new curriculum, set out in Clause 2, are:

> to prescribe a number of school subjects and specify in relation to each
> - knowledge, skills and understanding which pupils of different abilities and maturities are expected to have
> - matters, skills and processes which are required to be taught to pupils of different abilities and maturities
> - arrangements for assessing pupils

Core and other foundation subjects

All pupils are required to cover programmes of study in ten subjects.

Three of the subjects are defined as *core foundation* subjects and seven merely as *foundation* subjects. Most of the subjects are well known and have featured in school curricula for many years.

* English, mathematics, science	Core foundation subjects
* Art, geography, history, modern language, music, physical education, technology	Foundation subjects

All ten subjects must be taught through the compulsory years

---

* In Wales, Welsh is also taught as a core foundation subject where the medium of instruction in the school is Welsh. In all other Welsh schools, it is one of the foundation subjects.

of schooling. A modern language is the one exception. It is only compulsory at the secondary, 11+ level.

Schools are also required, as they always have been, to teach religious education. However, this is not one of the ten subjects of the National Curriculum, and arrangements for drawing up an agreed syllabus are made at the local education authority, not national level.

In the way the National Curriculum has developed there is little legal distinction between the *core foundation* and *foundation* subjects. The Secretary of State was required to introduce the three core subjects before any others, but the way the content is described is the same for each of the ten subjects. Four terms are used to describe each subject:

- Attainment targets
- Levels of attainment
- Statements of attainment
- Profile components

Attainment targets

Each subject is defined by *attainment targets* that all pupils must have the opportunity to study. In science, for example, there are seventeen such targets.

AT1   Exploration of science
AT2   The variety of life
AT3   Processes of life
AT4   Genetics and evolution
AT5   Human influences on the Earth
AT6   Types and uses of materials
AT7   Making new materials
AT8   Explaining how materials behave
AT9   Earth and atmosphere
AT10 Forces
AT11 Electricity and magnetism
AT12 The scientific aspects of information technology including microelectronics
AT13 Energy
AT14 Sound and music
AT15 Using light and electromagnetic radiation
AT16 The Earth in space
AT17 The nature of science

Levels of attainment

Each attainment target is subdivided into ten *levels of attainment*. Level one roughly corresponds to what might be achieved in the first year or so of schooling, and level ten to the upper secondary school years. In science attainment target 14 'Sound and music' the infant school pupil would be expected to 'know that sounds can be produced in a variety of ways', whilst the most advanced secondary school pupils would 'be able to apply knowledge of wave properties to explain common sound phenomena'.

The statements of attainment therefore provide the detail of what every pupil should know and understand as they progress through the curriculum. The attainment targets and the statements of attainment are central to the National Curriculum. The former act like the trunk of the tree, with the latter forming the branches. Every pupil should climb as high as they can. Look at the way this is set out in science for attainment target 14 'Sound and music'.

Attainment target 14: Sound and music

Pupils should develop their knowledge and understanding of the properties, transmission and absorption of sound.

LEVEL   STATEMENTS OF ATTAINMENT

Pupils should:

1
- know that sounds can be made in a variety of ways.

2
- know that sounds are heard when the sound reaches the ear.
- be able to explain how musical sounds are produced in simple musical instruments.

3
- know that sounds are produced by vibrating objects and can travel through different materials.
- be able to give a simple explanation of the way in which sound is generated and can travel through different materials.

4
- know that it takes time for sound to travel.

5
- understand that the frequency of a vibrating source affects the pitch of the sound it produces.
- understand the relationship between the loudness of a sound and the amplitude of vibration of the source.
- understand the importance of noise control in the environment.

6   • know that when sound waves travel from one point to
        another they transfer energy through the medium.
    • be able to explain the working of the human ear and some
        common defects in hearing.
    • be able to describe the working of audio devices, for
        example, *the microphone, loudspeaker and telephone.*

7   • know that sound waves can be converted into electrical
        oscillations, transmitted (as electrical, optical or radio
        signals) over long distances and converted into sound
        waves again.

8   • know that a vibrating object has a fundamental
        characteristic frequency of vibration, and that some
        systems produce resonant oscillations which can be
        advantageous or disadvantageous.

9   • understand the use of electronic sound technology, for
        example, *in industrial, medical and social applications.*

10 • be able to apply a knowledge of wave properties to
        explain common sound phenomena.

The number of statements of attainment at each level varies. As
the extract shows, there are three statements at each of levels 5
and 6, and one or two at the other levels. In other attainment
targets there are as many as ten statements or more at certain
levels.

It is important to realise that teachers will work to more than
one attainment target at a time. Many lessons or projects will
cover a series of targets. In science, for example, attainment
target 1 is about the process of scientific investigation, and aims
to develop the ability to:

(i)   plan, hypothesize and predict
(ii) design and carry out investigations
(iii) interpret results and findings
(iv) draw inferences
(v)   communicate exploratory tasks and experiments.

A teacher working on attainment target 14, 'Sound and music',
will be developing skills such as these simultaneously.

The targets and statements provide a framework against
which the teacher can check progress and ensure that impor-

tant areas are not missed. Learning within the National Curriculum could be compared to learning to ride a bike or drive a car: in practice a variety of skills have to be developed together. Every so often you may concentrate on just one, but always in the context of the others. You may also have to separate out the different techniques from time to time as a means of measuring progress and deciding where improvements can be made.

Programmes of study

The ways in which the attainment targets and statements of attainment are to be taught is set out in *programmes of study*. Teachers and schools are bound to follow these; they give more information to teachers about contents, methods and approaches. The programme of study for sound and music reads as follows:

> Children should have the opportunity to experience the range of sounds in their immediate environment and to find out about their causes and uses. They should investigate ways of making and experiencing sounds by vocalising and striking, plucking, shaking, scraping and blowing, for example, *using familiar objects and simple musical instruments from a variety of cultural traditions.* *
> Children should explore various ways of sorting these sounds and instruments.

So far, we have met three key terms which are used in National Curriculum statutory orders. The attainment targets and statements of attainment provide a structured shorthand that illustrates the scope of work required of pupils. Assessments, either by teachers or through externally-set tasks, will be made against these. Programmes of study are equally important for teachers implementing the National Curriculum, and you should refer to the published statutory orders (see Further reading) if you want to see them in full.

Profile components

The fourth important term is the *profile component*. The levels achieved by each child will be recorded against each attainment

---

* The parts of the programmes of study printed in italics do not represent a part of the statutory orders; they are not therefore a statutory requirement on schools.

target. When these are reported to parents, however, the scores will be clustered together in groups as a *profile component*. In science there are only two profile components and parents will therefore receive information about the levels achieved in each (see Section 5). All schools, eventually, will be able to give parents information about achievements on the different attainment targets leading up to an overall profile component score.

As far as the law is concerned, the attainment targets, statements of attainment, programmes of study and the profile components provide the backbone of the National Curriculum and they are laid down in statutory orders before parliament. They can be purchased from HMSO (see list of addresses on page 110).

Key stages

The law states what should be taught in stages, rather than in school years. The years 5–16 have been classified into four *key stages*, each covering two or three years of schooling:

Key Stage 1	5–7 year olds
Key Stage 2	9–11 year olds
Key Stage 3	11–14 year olds
Key Stage 4	14–16 year olds

An attempt is also being made to change the way teachers talk about year groups. At present, different systems are used in different parts of the country, and these can lead to confusion. For example, where middle schools exist, a pupil could move from year 5 in the middle school to year 3 in secondary or upper school. Schools are being recommended (although this is not obligatory) to describe the first infant year – where by the summer term the majority of children are 6 – as year 1, and then number through to the end of secondary schooling. Year 11 would describe the secondary school fifth form. The two sixth form years would become years 12 and 13. Many schools are using the new terms.

Key stage	New description	Age of majority of pupils at the end of the school year
	R*	5
1	Y1	6
	Y2	7
2	Y3	8
	Y4	9
	Y5	10
	Y6	11
3	Y7	12
	Y8	13
	Y9	14
4	Y10	15
	Y11	16
	Y12*	17
	Y13*	18

*Reception (R) and Y12–Y13 are not covered by National Curriculum legislation.

Using key stages as a structure, rather than ages or years, is a characteristic of the National Curriculum. For each subject, the range of levels that most children will work through is described. Examples for the core foundation subjects and technology are set out in the table below. The typical level of achievement at the end of each key stage is also shown.

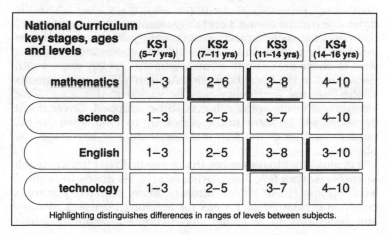

National Curriculum key stages, ages and levels	KS1 (5–7 yrs)	KS2 (7–11 yrs)	KS3 (11–14 yrs)	KS4 (14–16 yrs)
mathematics	1–3	2–6	3–8	4–10
science	1–3	2–5	3–7	4–10
English	1–3	2–5	3–8	3–10
technology	1–3	2–5	3–7	4–10

Highlighting distinguishes differences in ranges of levels between subjects.

This chart is only a guideline, based on what pupils of different ages achieve now in school. Many individual children will achieve higher levels than these average figures suggest. Over the coming years standards may change.

The programmes of study, attainment targets and statements of attainment around which teaching and learning are planned were initially established by working parties appointed by the Secretary of State. These produced reports which were the basis for consultation organised by the National Curriculum Council, which in turn makes recommendations about the way the statutory orders should be set out to the Secretary of State. At the end of the day, under the Education Reform Act, the form the final statutory orders laid before parliament take is a ministerial decision. There is an overall plan showing when the different subjects become part of the National Curriculum, and when they become a statutory requirement at the different key stages (see Section 9).

The Education Reform Act does not lay down for how long or for what percentage of the week each subject should be studied. Subsequent regulations only talk of providing a reasonable amount of time, which permits schools to organise their schemes of work to allow for worthwhile study by each pupil of the 'knowledge, skills and understanding, including processes, normally associated with the foundation subjects' (from a Department of Education and Science publication *National Curriculum: From Policy to Practice* distributed free to all teachers when the reforms were introduced).

There has been much speculation about how time should be divided up, especially at the upper secondary level where the timetable usually allows a certain percentage of time (about 10 per cent) for each subject. Responsibility for these decisions lies with the school, and in particular the governing board. It is wise to check the curriculum arrangements for key stage 4 with the school or the Local Education Authority. The requirements of the National Curriculum may be varied at this stage – for example, allowing some subjects to be dropped. Government decisions will be made in the period up to 1995 when the full implementation of the National Curriculum at key stage 4 is planned.

It is important to remember that schools do not have to teach in subjects. Very few, if any, primary schools divide the school week up into ten or eleven subjects. Many secondary schools combine certain subject areas for teaching purposes. History and geography, for example, may become humanities, music and art may be part of an overall arts provision that includes dance and drama. There is no reason to stop doing this, provided attention is given to the content of the National Curriculum subject areas and provided, where programmes of study, attainment targets and statements of attainment are laid down in statutory orders, that the requirements are met. There are many ways in which schools can set out to do this. The particular style and approach chosen has to be agreed by the school governors, who in turn report to parents. Information about the curriculum must also be given in the school prospectus. Section 8 explains these requirements in some detail.

Whatever the structure of the curriculum, there is a further dimension to the National Curriculum that both primary and secondary schools will have to incorporate in their plans. This is the area of *cross curricular themes,* about which there has been much debate since the first publication of a National Curriculum consultative document in 1987. If the curriculum is described in terms of subjects, there is a danger that many important elements of a whole curriculum plan are neglected. Examples include personal and social education, health education, environment education or economic and industrial understanding. Schools should be able to show how each of these is represented in the curriculum. The guidance given to schools by the national councils stresses the significance of these curricular areas, not least in terms of the way that each evolves throughout the child's total school career.

It is important to remember that the National Curriculum does not cover the whole of the school curriculum. Children will study subjects and take part in activities which are additional to those set out in statutory orders. The school prospectus will indicate the variety and range of the whole curriculum offered.

SECTION 2

Why a National Curriculum?

Advocates of a National Curriculum can be found right across the political spectrum. It is highly unlikely that changes in government would lead to the total repeal of the legislation, and the signs are that a National Curriculum will be part of the educational scene for the foreseeable future.

Differences between schools

For many educationists the logic that underpins the provision of free and compulsory schooling also extends to what is taught. In arguing for a National Curriculum, they point to glaring inconsistencies between schools. In the same locality, one primary school may have had a fully worked out science scheme, and another school no science scheme at all. Even if both schools did have plans for teaching science, there would be no guarantee that they would approach the subject in similar ways. One school might have attempted to achieve a balance between the different scientific disciplines (physics, chemistry, biology and perhaps astronomy and earth sciences). The other, however, could have leaned heavily on the tradition of nature study – the sort of primary science that most parents remember from their own school days. In other subjects similar differences existed. A survey by Her Majesty's Inspectorate at the end of the 1980s showed how haphazard the teaching of history and geography could be. They pointed to the lack of any attempt in many schools to ensure that children came into contact with progressively more demanding ideas, skills and concepts.

Inequality of provision

In secondary schools the existence of different curriculum opportunities could be seen clearly. Girls, for example, often chose to drop the physical sciences in favour of biology. Boys significantly outnumbered girls in the technology classes that became increasingly available in the decade prior to the passing of the 1988 Education Reform Act. In a similar way, boys had very little contact with home economics. There were also some anomalies that affected both boys and girls. A high proportion of pupils dropped the learning of a foreign language in the final two years of schooling. An even bigger proportion – perhaps as high as 90 per cent – had no musical education in the final two years of compulsory schooling. A National Curriculum provides a framework that, in theory, rules out such inconsistencies and inequalities in provision. Pupils and their parents now have access to public documents that describe the subjects and content to be covered at each stage of development.

Raising standards

Many supporters of the National Curriculum are also motivated by the desire to improve the quality of schooling and raise standards. The debate over standards has attracted media interest and controversy for many years. Some people have perceived a fall in standards of attainment in subjects such as English and mathematics. This is vigorously refuted by others, who point to the regular improvements in examination performance of both sixteen and eighteen year-olds, particularly in the 1960s and 1980s. For example, in 1970–71 16.6 per cent of the age group left school with one or more GCE A levels. By 1984–85 that percentage had increased to 18.1 per cent. In the same period the number of young people leaving school without A levels but with five or more higher grades at GCE/CSE or equivalent rose from 7.1 per cent to 10.3 per cent. Those with between one and four higher grades at GCE/CSE or equivalent rose from 16.9 per cent to 26.8 per cent, and those with one or more graded results rose from 9.8 per cent to 32.5 per cent. Those with no graded results fell from 44 per cent to 11.7 per cent. These comparisons have been taken from official DES statistics.

There are also reports from the Assessment of Performance Unit, set up in 1978 to monitor the extent to which standards vary over time. The work done by the unit shows how difficult a task this is. Knowledge is always evolving, and therefore the sort of tasks and questions that are appropriate in one decade may be redundant in the next. Extending the comparisons over more than a decade gives even greater difficulties. Changes in language usage make comparisons in English difficult. In mathematics the pounds, shillings and pence sums familiar to many parents could hardly be set today.

Despite the complexity and inconclusiveness of the debate, a political and media message about declining standards achieved widespread public acceptance. More than one Prime Minister has chosen to exploit the issue for political advantage. James Callaghan, in a famous speech at Ruskin College, Oxford in 1976, talked of his concern at finding 'complaints from industry that new recruits from the schools sometimes do not have the basic tools to do the job that is required'. Margaret Thatcher in her 1987 speech to the Conservative Party Conference made a direct link between schooling and economic success: 'To compete successfully in tomorrow's world – against Japan, Germany and the United States – we need well-educated, well-trained, creative young people. If education is backward today, national performance will be backward tomorrow.'

International comparisons represent a further dimension of the standards debate. Yet again, there are difficulties in coming to conclusive judgements. Setting tests that are comparable across a range of different countries and cultures has proved highly controversial. Assessments of practical and investigative work in science, for example, increasingly a feature of British science education, would be inappropriate in a different educational system where most teaching was through books and academic exercises. Some comparisons have been made that show how in mathematics and some aspects of science, British pupils do not attain as highly as their Japanese equivalents. A 1988 publication by the International Associates for the Evaluation of Educational Achievement, *Science Achievement in Seventeen Countries*, showed that this was particularly true in the initial stages of secondary education, where England is listed with Hong Kong, Italy, Singapore and the USA. These are all countries which the report says should be concerned about 'the scientific literacy of their general workforce'. Finland, Hungary, Japan and Sweden led the field in mass secondary science attainment. The same report, however, shows how at more advanced levels, Hong Kong, England and Singapore together with Hungary and Japan would appear to be educating their elite relatively well.

Other research (opposite) shows British performance in mathematics to be around the mean of a range of countries where testing took place. The Centre for the Assessment of Educational Progress in the USA looked at average mathematics proficiency for thirteen year-olds, and came to the conclusion that the South Koreans were the highest attainers, with the USA at the bottom of the league.

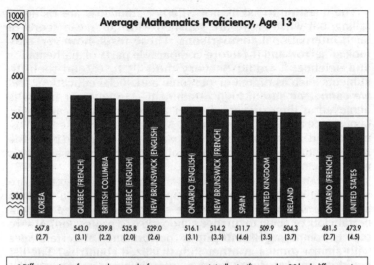

Average Mathematics Proficiency, Age 13*

KOREA	QUEBEC (FRENCH)	BRITISH COLUMBIA	QUEBEC (ENGLISH)	NEW BRUNSWICK (ENGLISH)	ONTARIO (ENGLISH)	NEW BRUNSWICK (FRENCH)	SPAIN	UNITED KINGDOM	IRELAND	ONTARIO (FRENCH)	UNITED STATES
567.8	543.0	539.8	535.8	529.0	516.1	514.2	511.7	509.9	504.3	481.5	473.9
(2.7)	(3.1)	(2.2)	(2.0)	(2.6)	(3.1)	(3.3)	(4.6)	(3.5)	(3.7)	(2.7)	(4.5)

* Differences in performance between the four groups are statistically significant at the .05 level; differences in performance within groups are not statistically significant. Jackknifed standard errors are presented in parentheses.

In Science, the United Kingdom's record is slightly better.

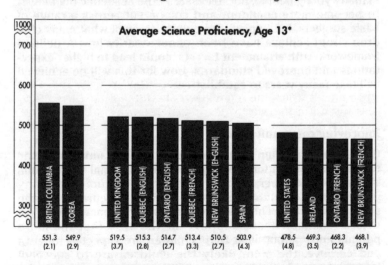

Average Science Proficiency, Age 13*

BRITISH COLUMBIA	KOREA	UNITED KINGDOM	QUEBEC (ENGLISH)	ONTARIO (ENGLISH)	QUEBEC (FRENCH)	NEW BRUNSWICK (ENGLISH)	SPAIN	UNITED STATES	IRELAND	ONTARIO (FRENCH)	NEW BRUNSWICK (FRENCH)
551.3	549.9	519.5	515.3	514.7	513.4	510.5	503.9	478.5	469.3	468.3	468.1
(2.1)	(2.9)	(3.7)	(2.8)	(2.7)	(3.3)	(2.7)	(4.3)	(4.8)	(3.5)	(2.2)	(3.9)

* Differences in performance between the three groups are statistically significant at the .05 level; differences in performance within groups are not statistically significant. Jackknifed standard errors are presented in parentheses.

The question to ask is not whether standards are rising or falling, but whether we are satisfied with the 'mean score' of such international comparisons. These tests, however, only look at narrow and therefore comparable parts of mathematics and science. It would be very difficult to extend them to subjects such as drama or personal and social education. And we cannot be sure if high attainment in science or maths is achieved at the expense of other areas of school learning or experience that we value highly. Methods of teaching mathematics and science in Korea or Japan do not appear to place the same emphasis on developing problem solving skills as in this country.

As we can see, the question of standards is a complex one. Are we talking about attainment in specified subjects at certain ages? Are we thinking about the standards required to do a certain job, or go on to further schooling or a profession? Are we merely comparing British pupils' performance at certain ages with similar groups in other industrialized countries? The list could go on. Are there, for example, differences between the north of the country and the south-east? How significant are urban and rural comparisons? The most important point to bear in mind when thinking of a National Curriculum is the potential of many young people, not necessarily the academic high fliers, to become more confident and competent across a range of basic subjects. In the past, the expectations of what many children could achieve have been unnecessarily low. A defined framework, with attainment targets, could lead to higher expectations and improved standards. How far this will be achieved will take many years to establish.

Improving communication

Creating a curriculum entitlement and raising standards are the two major justifications for a prescribed National Curriculum. There are, however, further supporting arguments. Many parents have found the curriculum a rather obscure part of the school's activities. There is some research evidence and a good deal of common sense support for the view that the more parents know about what their children are expected to learn and achieve, the more likely the children are to succeed. Information such as this has been difficult for parents to obtain, not because of any obstruction on the part of teachers, but because there was no common language or agreed structure within which to explain or report on children's progress. Even where examination syllabuses existed, for GCSE or A level for example, parents could find it difficult to ascertain even roughly what point in the syllabus their child had reached. In many instances pupils would sit the examination without ever having seen the syllabus! The National Curriculum, with its relatively straightforward terminology, provides the basis for greater clarity in school-parent communication at both primary and secondary level.

Progress and continuity

The National Curriculum is an important means of improving the links between primary and secondary schools. Despite the existence of many well organized liaison schemes, there has been much concern about the problems of transfer from primary to secondary schools. Secondary teachers receiving pupils from different primary schools have found it difficult to establish the subject content previously covered, or the level of attainment reached by individual children. It was not unusual for some secondary teachers to talk about 'starting from scratch'. This was particularly problematic in subjects where knowledge tends to build up sequentially, for example in mathematics, science, and perhaps music. A research study from the University of Leicester showed children actually falling back in attainment when moving schools. The National Curriculum provides a focus for better record-keeping and monitoring of progress between teachers and between schools.

All these arguments apply equally where forms of schooling other than primary and secondary exist. In some areas the existence of middle schools, or junior high schools, means that children have two changes of school, rather than the more usual one. Many families have to move from place to place because of job opportunities. Even within the same school, teachers move to new posts, fall ill, or are involved in in-service training. These events can lead to significant breaks in the continuity of children's education. Again, the National Curriculum is a means of minimizing disruption.

Individual attainment

Finally, there is one major potential advantage of the National Curriculum that could radically change the way school-days are experienced. Many parents will remember the monthly or termly 'position in class' lists compiled by form teachers. Similar lists were drawn up to describe the end-of-term examination results. Grading schemes might also have been used; in many schools A-E for attainment and 1–5 for effort was widely adopted in the 1970s and 1980s. Most of these schemes involved ranking pupils one against the other. In fact, this has been the major form of assessment in British schooling for most of this century. Inevitably, a large proportion of pupils must come out as below average.

Rank order is most significant when it determines access to limited places, for example at universities or the administrative grades of the Civil Service. The public examination system served this purpose for most of this century. The eleven-plus examination, which selected about 20 per cent of the age group to go on to a grammar school education is one of the best known examples of rank ordering. The statistical model upon which the tests and examinations were based was the bell curve, with the bulk of the population (average performance) found at the top of the curve, and the most or least able on the extremities.

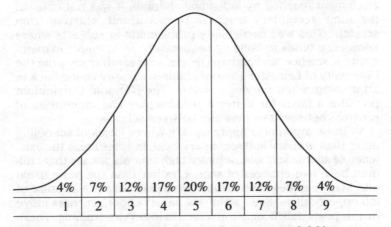

4%	7%	12%	17%	20%	17%	12%	7%	4%
1	2	3	4	5	6	7	8	9

Classical statistical representation, showing the proportions of children expected at each level of performance.

Many of those who have advocated a National Curriculum argue that we should be moving away from standards based on relative information (how you compare with others) to absolute standards (whether you have shown individual knowledge and competency in the different parts of the curriculum). Everyone should be able to achieve the higher levels of attainment, it is argued. The government-appointed Task Group on Assessment and Performance, set up to work out how the National Curriculum should be assessed, made this very clear in the second report they produced. They said that the proposals should be confined to 'the assessment of "performance" or "attainment" and [they] were not recommending any attempt to assess separately the problematic notion of underlying "ability".'

This represents something of a challenge to school organizations where ranking still lives on. For the most part the 'position in class' lists have disappeared, but in teachers' and parents' minds the old idea, discredited by many of the developments in psychology, that children are born with a fixed potential remains. The National Curriculum provides a national yardstick against which unrecognized potential can be realized and acknowledged.

The National Curriculum
in the classroom

Much of the work done in classrooms today will reflect the way teaching has evolved over many years. The look of the primary classroom as parents wait to collect their children at the end of the school day is very much the same as in pre-National Curriculum days, with children putting away books and pens, clearing up art materials or perhaps tidying the reading corner. The teacher might be asking two children to tell the rest of the class tomorrow morning about the plants they are growing in the school garden. In secondary schools, pupils will almost certainly have spent the day moving from one specialist area to another. Homework will have been set in certain of the core and foundation subjects. Some classes may have been asked to interview their parents about 'school-day memories' as part of a project in English. In many schools such a project will involve links with the history department. Sometimes there will have been class-centred lessons, with a teacher introducing a part of the scheme of work or syllabus and the pupils following this up with individual exercises or note-taking. In other classes, design tasks in technology, experiments in science or a problem-solving exercise in mathematics may have involved pupils working together in groups of three or four.

The changes brought in by the National Curriculum which do affect teaching and classrooms can be summarized as follows:

- The way the curriculum is described is similar in primary and secondary schools. Programmes of study, attainment targets and levels of attainment follow, as we have seen, right through the compulsory years of schooling.
- Each school and therefore each teacher now has the basis for a scheme of work which shows how the curriculum meets the requirements of the National Curriculum. These are public documents that parents have the right to examine (see Section 8).
- There will be more recording of the work done in the class-room. Teachers will be looking to record which attainment

targets have been covered and the level at which individual children are working. These records will form the basis for discussions with parents about the progress achieved.

- In many, perhaps all schools, the children will be encouraged to record their own progress through the schemes of work. Parents, for example, in talking to their children should be able to keep closely in touch with progress in between the regular meetings with class or subject teachers.
- In primary schools a great deal more science will now be taught, and this will include elements of all the major disciplines.
- In primary and secondary schools new programmes of technology have been introduced, incorporating elements of subjects such as craft, design and technology, business studies, home economics and information technology.
- At the secondary level all pupils will now study a modern language probably through to the age of sixteen.
- In all schools teachers will have made plans to cover topics such as health education or career guidance through the schemes of work. Schools are not required by law to implement these cross-curricular themes, but are strongly encouraged to do so in guidance and advice from the National Curriculum Council.
- Standard Assessment Tasks are used to check progress in the National Curriculum and to ensure that teachers' assessments are in line with nationally-agreed standards. The tasks are intended to be built around normal classroom teaching approaches and are intended to blend with day-to-day teaching plans.

The following examples show how the National Curriculum attainment targets are used in teaching. The first example is from a primary school (with the teacher working at key stage 1), and the second is from the early years of secondary education (with the teacher working at key stage 3).

My day yesterday – topic work in the primary school (key stage 1)

In this example the teacher began with a familiar activity. The children were asked to write down everything they had done the day before, including what they had eaten, the time they went to bed and so forth. Some of the children used few words and drew cartoon type pictures of the events of the day.

The teacher then brought the class into a circle and the children began to talk about which events in the day were common and on which occasions someone had done something different to all the others. The teacher used the information recorded by the children as a starting point for a series of activities covering many parts of the National Curriculum.

In the core foundation subjects the attainment targets (ATs) in English for 'Speaking and listening' and 'Writing' were clearly addressed by the activity. For example, in AT1 'Speaking and listening' one statement of attainment at level 2,

- Describe briefly an event to the teacher or another pupil

was touched on by the whole class and in groups. AT3 at the same level includes a statement that children should be able to

- Structure sequences of real or imagined events coherently in chronological accounts.

It is also stated that children should

- produce independently short pieces of writing using complete sentences, some demarcated with capital letters and full stops or question marks.

In planning this activity, therefore, the teacher thought specifically of these statements although others within the statutory order would also be covered. Teachers frequently have a specific focus for a learning activity and the statements of attainment act like cues as to what this might be. The teacher is free, however, to explore issues and topics outside the National Curriculum. In this class one of the children described her mother's work as a policewoman. She had come home from duty just before he went to bed and told him about a government minister visiting the town. The teacher used this to talk about the police and government. The children drew pictures of incidents they remembered involving policemen and policewomen. Books from the class and school library were brought in. The initial idea for the topic had extended to incorporate activities the teacher could not have anticipated. A few days later, the policewoman came to the school and talked about her job to the whole class.

As the week progressed, the teacher developed the theme to cover other subjects. In science, for example, all primary children are expected to know and understand something about the organization of living things and the processes which characterize their survival and reproduction. Statements of attainment are set out under AT3 'Process of life', and at level 2 pupils are expected to know and understand three statements, two of which are relevant to the topic 'My day yesterday'.

At this level all children should:

- know that personal hygiene, food, exercise, rest and safety, and the proper and safe use of medicines are important
- be able to give a simple account of the pattern of their own day.

In AT1 'Exploration of science', children should be able to

- record findings in charts, drawings and other appropriate forms.

The topic provided plenty of opportunity for the teacher to develop work in all three areas. It was also linked to mathematics, where for example AT14 'Handling data' says pupils should

- choose criteria to sort and classify objects; record results of observations or outcomes of events
- help to design a data collection sheet and use it to record a set of data leading to a frequency table.

In the next attainment target, which looks at the representation and interpretation of data, all children at level 2 should be able to

- construct, read and interpret block graphs and frequency tables.

In the Statutory orders, examples of classroom activities are given such as identifying children who walk to school and those who travel by bus or car. This information, when collected, can be represented easily in bar graph form.

Teachers will continuously make decisions about how wide-ranging or restricted the topics could be. In the 'My day yesterday' topic, the teacher chose not to highlight the weather! This could have been included, however, and the children focused on the science AT9, 'Earth and atmosphere' which at the second level says that children should

- know that the weather has a powerful effect on people's lives.

The teacher did introduce activities that helped develop skills in language, in science and in mathematics. She was also able to develop activities that arose from the children's own accounts. Artwork was also featured in the topic.

The National Curriculum Council has recognized the importance of primary curriculum planning across subjects and the different attainment targets. In the first booklet of Curriculum Guidance, *A Framework for the Primary Curriculum*, it said

> 'The National Curriculum Council recognises that in primary schools a range of work takes place which is described as "thematic", "topic based" or "cross-curricular" in nature. It would be counter-productive to lose existing good practice and unhelpful for the learner to devise an unnecessarily fragmented curriculum.'

In the same report the Council shows how language work in topics can be developed through mathematics and science. It lists, for example, the statements of attainment at level 2 in science, English and mathematics that show possibilities for collaboration, through working across the subjects.

Statements of attainment

SCIENCE	ENGLISH	MATHEMATICS
Level 2		
Ask questions and suggest ideas of the 'how' and 'why' and 'what will happen if' variety	Respond appropriately to a range of more complex instructions given by a teacher and give simple instructions.	Ask and respond to the question, 'What would happen if . . . ?'
Record findings in charts, drawings and other appropriate forms.	Produce simple, coherent non-chronological writing.	Describe current work, record findings and check results.
Be able to keep a diary, in a variety of forms, of change over time.	Structure sequences of real or imagined events coherently in chronological accounts.	Help to design a data collection sheet and use it to record a set of data leading to a frequency table.

At secondary level, the same approach to planning is developed, although the starting point is more likely to be through subjects.

Volcanoes and earthquakes – a secondary science project

Many people will remember studying volcanoes at school. It may have been in a science, geography, or even history lesson. Drawing a cross-section of an active volcano and hearing accounts of famous eruptions such as Krakatoa seem to stay long in most people's minds. The science statutory orders cover this through attainment target 9, 'Earth and atmosphere'. The chart below shows the statements of attainment at Level 5.

AT9   Earth and atmosphere

Level 5 • be able to explain how earthquakes and volcanoes are associated with the formation of landforms.

The teacher has planned a series of lessons around this topic. The children begin by reading an account of the San Francisco earthquake of 1906, and the more recent one in 1989. They then use a slide sequence that describes the eruption of Vesuvius.

This provides the starting point for a run of activities planned around a chapter in the textbook that looks at volcanoes and earthquakes in the context of other attainment targets in science.

For example, pupils learn about the Richter scale for measuring the intensity of an earthquake as set out in the second part of the statement of attainment below.

AT1   Exploration of science

Level 5 • select and use measuring instruments to quantify variables and use more complex measuring instruments with the required degree of accuracy, for example, minor divisions on thermometers and forcemeters.

The teacher would be able to introduce similar, direct links with attainment target 10, 'Forces', attainment target 13, 'Energy', and attainment target 14, 'Sound and music'.

Schools plan the National Curriculum to maximize the cross-references that could be made to other subjects. The science teacher, for example, would be aware of English and mathematics attainment targets at level 5. The description of volcanic eruptions and earthquakes would develop English skills. Skills of data interpretation would be developed by looking at seismic graphs. The final part of this series of lessons is jointly taught by the class teachers of science and technology. The technology teacher has acquired a video that shows how high-rise buildings in places like San Francisco and Tokyo are constructed to withstand earth tremors and earthquakes.

SECTION 4

Testing and assessment
in the National Curriculum

Testing and assessment is the issue that provokes the greatest controversy amongst educationists, parents and the public generally. For pupils it can be one of the most worrying aspects of school life. It is also ultimately one of the most important. Tests, assessments and examinations are a significant factor in determining job prospects or access to college or higher education. If you want to be a vet, the very highest grades at Advanced (A level) will be required. No one can become a teacher without obtaining General Certificates of Secondary Education (GCSE) in English and mathematics at grades A to C. A levels are also required.

The National Curriculum is accompanied by national assessments that begin at an early age. Previously most pupils, apart from taking reading tests, were well into secondary schooling before they came into contact with a nationally standardized examination. Now a measurement is being made from the age of seven about the levels reached and progress made. Many parents support this idea. Opinion polls continually show a majority in favour. This isn't surprising. Most people expect some sort of feedback about how well their children are doing.

Immediately, however, problems begin to arise. Testing children to see how much they know appears to many people a straightforward process. In Section 2 the difficulty of monitoring standards was explained. Producing fair and reliable ways of testing children is equally difficult, and the government has spent millions of pounds on research projects in attempting to solve the problems.

Assessment is full of jargon, and before explaining the issues and methods being used, we need to explain some of it. Firstly, is there any difference between the terms 'tests', 'assessment' and 'examinations'? In practice the answer is no. All three terms are used interchangeably. Distinctions have begun to emerge, however, and in talking to teachers you may begin to detect signs of this. Tests now tend to be seen as limited activities, perhaps involving spelling or mental arithmetic, that contribute to the ongoing process of assessing. Examinations are usually seen as final, marking the end of the year or the end of the school process. Most commonly now, they are associated with public examinations such as GCSEs or A levels. The term assessment, however, covers tests, examinations and all the other ways in which teachers check and monitor progress.

In schools now, the most significant term is assessment. This has two important sub-categories within the National Curriculum.

Firstly there is *continuous assessment* by the teacher or teachers. This is the daily and weekly record in all aspects of the curriculum organized by the teacher and transferred on to individual record cards. Every so often the teacher will look at the detailed records of progress and make a judgement about the level of work being achieved by the child.

Secondly there are *standard assessment tasks*. These are written and set outside the school by organizations commissioned by the Schools Examinations and Assessment Council. At different stages during the school year, children at certain ages will be involved in activities within which the standard assessment tasks have been built. At the primary stage compulsory standard assessment tasks will be restricted to core subjects (English, mathematics, science). How well the children complete the tasks will be recorded and compared with the judgement being made by the teachers through the continuous assessment process. This should allow the teachers to check that they are in line with nationally agreed standards.

Teachers use all sorts of ways of recording assessment continuously. They will take information from written work, from children's answers to questions and from the way the children perform practical tasks individually or in a group. The standard assessment tasks (frequently called SATs) contain a similar variety of activities but these have been trialled and piloted with hundreds of children to ensure they give reliable information about the level children can achieve.

How continuous assessment works

Teachers are unable to assess all the children in their class all the time. As the year progresses, therefore, it is likely that they will give particular attention to two or three children at a time. In the last section we saw some primary teaching focusing initially at AT1 'Speaking and listening' and AT3 'Writing'. In continuously assessing, the teacher could on one day:

- Have individual conversations with four or five children to see that they could briefly describe an event from the previous day. The teacher will be experienced in judging whether the child is confident in doing this (in which case a note will be made in the child's record) or whether further practice is needed (in which case the teacher may suggest an activity in the group where the child can practice further). The teacher would also make a mental (or perhaps written) note to have another conversation later in the week in which an event can be described briefly.
- After school, the teacher may spend some time looking at the written work completed by all the children. She would be looking particularly for evidence of sentences with capital letters and full stops. AT3 at level 2 includes this as a statement of attainment that all children should strive towards. As she looks at the books the teacher would make a note against each child's record. It is unlikely that a judgement would be made about whether the child was fully competent on the basis of one piece of written work. The teacher will have built up a knowledge of each child over the year and will use a variety of evidence in making a final assessment.

The secondary science teacher working on volcanoes and earthquakes will be involved in a similar process.

- In this class the teacher is using a recording system that allows her to note when pupils are successful with practical activities. In science classes today there are few occasions on which all children are asked to do the same activity, then stop and wait to have their work marked by the teacher. More commonly they carry out experiments and the teacher observes different parts of the process to see how well they are doing. During one week's lessons, therefore, the teacher may observe all the groups and make judgements about pupils' competency in using measuring instruments with a reasonable degree of accuracy (AT1, 'Exploration of science', level 5).
- In the same class the teacher may set a written assignment, following reading and discussion in class, that provides evidence of the child's understanding about the different sources of raw material (air, water, rocks, living things, fossil fuels) that are used in manufacture (AT7).

    The teacher's written comments in the children's exercise books would indicate how well they had done and how, if necessary, they could go over the work again (or follow it up in a different way) to achieve a fresh understanding of the concept. Depending on how well the group as a whole had done, the teacher could decide:

to do something with the whole class on this,
to follow up the concept with a group of pupils,
　or
to give some individual help as the vast majority had clearly grasped what was involved.

Every so often teachers will take their records and make judgements about the level being achieved against each of the attainment targets they are covering. This is the information used to produce the profile component scores that will be given to parents along with all the other information about how hard their child is working, whether they seem to be enjoying the subject, how regularly homework is being completed, and so forth. Parents may also wish to ask about the sort of recording system being used daily. Schools will be explaining this at parents' evenings or at special events to describe the way the National Curriculum works in practice. Each school has established their own daily and class record scheme, following advice from national organizations like the Schools Examinations and Assessment Council and the National Curriculum Council, as well as from local advisers or inspectors.

The new approach to assessment

The sort of assessment that merely gives you a grade (like a formal public examination) tells you very little about which parts of the syllabus you did well on or where you went wrong. Giving you a position in a class list is much the same; all you can tell from the list is how you compare with others. The new approach to assessment attempts to do four things.

- Firstly, it attempts to recognise when children have achieved a target, to acknowledge this in a positive way, and then to help them plan the next stages of learning.

This is called *formative* assessment.

- Secondly, the assessment process aims to reveal weaknesses or difficulties in such a way that appropriate help can be given and the child can overcome the problem.

This is termed the *diagnostic* purpose of assessment.

This reflects the way most people learn. Initially you experience patchy understanding. You need to spot your areas of weakness and remedy them through extra work and attention. The driving test, for example, tries to be diagnostic in that you are given feedback on the specific parts of the test you fail. As you trek back sadly to your friendly instructor for further lessons, it would serve little purpose merely to announce that you had a D fail grade! The detailed recording and judgements involved in teachers' continuous assessment should, if working well, provide important formative and diagnostic information for every child.

It is worth emphasising that the aim is TO SHOW THE CHILD WHAT HE OR SHE HAS ACHIEVED, not where they have failed!

- Thirdly, the assessment process aims to give teachers, the child and parents an overall summary of what has been achieved, at regular intervals.

This is termed the *summative* purpose of assessment.

In the National Curriculum the summary is made on the basis of the levels of attainment reached in the attainment targets of the different subjects. This is discussed in greater detail later in the section.

- Fourthly, the results of these assessments are used by teachers, headteachers and governors to see how well they are doing against the targets they will have established for the school as a whole.

This could be called the *evaluative* purpose of evaluation.

Reports on overall achievements for every school are made available to everyone in the form of public documents.

In the examples of classroom activities in Section 3 you will have seen how the teacher can use assessment for formative and diagnostic purposes. This is, of course, nothing new. The best teachers have always used a similar approach. The National Curriculum has given an added impetus to this, and in particular the chance to make assessment a positive experience for the child. Two further phrases help explain this more clearly.

The old system of assessment was almost wholly *norm referenced*. In the Secondary Examinations and Assessment Council's *Guide to Teacher Assessment* this is defined as

'a system in which pupils are placed in rank order, and (often) pre-determined proportions are placed in the various grades. It implies that grades are assigned by comparison to other pupils' performance, rather than upon the absolute quality of the performance.'

The idea of pre-determined proportions was considered in Section 2. The 'bell curve' was, and in many examinations still is used to allocate grades. The great difficulty with norm referencing is that a proportion of pupils are inevitably deemed to have done badly, and come away with a negative experience not only of the examination or test but of school generally.

The alternative to norm referencing is termed *criterion-referencing,* and it is this that the National Curriculum assessments attempt to achieve. The definition given in the *Guide to Teacher Assessment* is

'a system where a pupil's achievements are judged in relation to objectives, irrespective of other pupils' performance.'

As we have seen, if the pupil shows competency against different statements of attainment then he or she will be deemed to have achieved success. The driving test is often used as an example of criterion-referencing. Success or failure depends on a display of competency against specified criteria. In the National Curriculum, Standard Assessment Tests (SATS) are being developed to measure individual achievement against specified criteria.

The acronym SATS has now entered into educational folklore. Through most of the early part of the 1990s different groups of people, including University departments, publishers and private organizations have been beavering away trying to develop valid and reliable assessments or SATS against which the accuracy of the teacher's assessment can be measured. It is proving an extremely difficult and complex task, and many strong criticisms have been made of some of the first attempts. For example, some SATS have provided what appears to be accurate information about children's progress, but in doing so have produced bewilderingly detailed information for parents. On the other hand, where simple information has been produced, the validity and reliability is drawn into question.

In early 1990 the Secretary of State for education announced that the SATS for key stages 1 and 2 would be likely to cover only the core foundation subjects of English, mathematics and science. This was a significant change from the original plans. Until the development projects are complete, it is impossible to give an accurate description of even a sample national assessment. Many different types are being piloted. In primary schools the assessments being piloted usually cover a number of subject areas. It is likely that a small number of SATs in the core subjects will be compulsory, with schools free to use others for different parts of the curriculum, if they wish. In secondary schools, for key stages 3 and 4, the first development work is more subject-centred.

Inevitably this aspect of National Curriculum assessment has aroused considerable interest and, amongst teachers and parents, not a little apprehension. It is important to remember that the first reported and compulsory assessments for seven year-olds will not appear until the summer of 1992, and for eleven year-olds the summer of 1995. Fourteen and sixteen year-olds are planned to have assessment in the core subjects in 1993 or 1994 (see Section 9). Firstly, until these assessments are in place, teachers' descriptions of children's levels of achievement can only be tentative. They may be using the National Curriculum system of levels, but the reliability and validity of the judgements will not have been ascertained. Secondly, there have been difficulties in producing SATS and we may have to wait a number of years before final versions emerge. The indications are that the testing and assessment will be nowhere near as extensive as was first envisaged. Whatever form of assessment finally emerges will depend on teachers being trained in the new procedures. Particular emphasis is likely to be given to teachers visiting other schools and comparing the judgements they are making with others in the locality. This process of moderation, common practice in the exam year of the secondary school, will become increasingly common in the primary and lower secondary years.

Many people also wonder about the relationship between National Curriculum assessments and GCSE. The plan is that the higher levels of the National Curriculum will equate with the A–F grading system used for GCSE. However, it is still unclear how this will be worked out and again, it is best not to try and guess about controversial decisions for the future.

Alongside teachers' continuous assessment, SATs and the GCSE, there has been another development that has had an impact on a great many schools. Originally this began in secondary schools, but an increasing number of primary schools are adopting the idea. *Records of achievement* were first planned in the 1970s and early 1980s, to give much greater acknowledgement to what young people achieved in school. The vast majority of secondary school leavers had very little to show for their efforts and enthusiasm across the broad range of school life. Examination results gave an indication of academic attainment, but what about all the other qualities that schools have a responsibility to develop?

Achievements in creative activities, the school play or other aspect of drama, music and dance gained little recognition. Sporting achievement may have gained passing recognition, but there was no ongoing record that the pupils could take away with them. And then there are the host of other pursuits that the good school fosters: outdoor pursuits, community help programmes and charity fund-raising, to give just three examples. Only in a very few schools had these been systematically recorded.

A great many schools now use a 'record of achievement'. The form and style will vary from area to area, but most aim to record achievements in all aspects of school life. Some also record important achievements outside school. It is usually the pupil who is responsible for compiling and collating the record, helped by a form teacher or counsellor. Most records contain information about academic work as well, including eventually grades obtained in examinations. Achievements on the way to public examinations are as important as the final grades, and nearly all records of achievement recognise this. Many young people choose to use their record at interviews with potential employers or when transferring to other forms of education. It is also the document to be kept at home, treasured, and years later shown with some pride to the grandchildren!

There is no legal requirement to provide a record of achievement, although the government is supportive of the principles involved. The 1988 Education Reform Act does however make some aspects of assessment statutory, and it is important to note these.

Section 4(2) of the Education Reform Act allows the Secretary of State to specify attainment targets and programmes of study in the National Curriculum. At other places in the Act there is specific reference to assessment, records and reporting. The plans for how schools are to implement the reformed system are not in the Act, but are contained in orders and regulations issued by the Secretary of State following discussion and consultation. There is now a clear requirement for schools to give an annual report to parents on the progress being made by their child. This will involve information about levels achieved, backed up by a written report. A good school will support this with a personal interview. The teacher-training materials produced by SEAC strongly advocated a collaborative approach between parents and teachers in reviewing the work of the child. Parents, they point out, should

> 'have access to the detailed picture of the child's progress, of where the progress is rapid and where that progress is slow. Sensitively handled there is an excellent opportunity for the creation of a helpful and supportive relationship between teacher, parent and pupil.'

The way class and school assessments are reported is explained in Section 8, which looks in more detail at parents and the National Curriculum.

To summarize, therefore, National Curriculum assessments are intended to be very different from the sort of paper and pencil tests that most adults experienced in school. However, they do provide a check on how hard someone has been working! In addition, they should:

- give credit for hard work and achievement;
- point out gaps or weaknesses that, independently or with the teacher, can be remedied;
- indicate realistically what can be attempted next;
- record an individual's specific attainments and performance.

Parents will receive plenty of guidance from teachers and schools about how to interpret the increased variety of information available to them.

SECTION 5

The core foundation subjects of the National Curriculum:

English, mathematics and science

The Education Reform Act specified these three subjects as the central focus of the National Curriculum. Programmes of study and attainment targets for each were devised and introduced before any of the other subjects. This isn't surprising. English and mathematics have provided the mainstay of the curriculum in both primary and secondary schools for many years. Increasingly, science has been recognized as so important that every child should follow a compulsory course. The difficulty, as Section 1 explored, has been the diversity of science courses at the primary level (with some schools having none at all to speak of) and the way many pupils dropped science courses when they began GCSE. The National Curriculum now gives everyone the entitlement to a science course from the age of five through to sixteen.

English

There are five attainment targets for English:

AT1	Speaking and listening	
AT2	Reading	
AT3	Writing	
AT4	Spelling	} After level 4 these become one
AT5	Handwriting	} attainment target, 'Presentation'.

For reporting purposes – that is the way in which assessment must, by law, be recorded and notified to parents – these targets are grouped into three profile components. AT1 and AT2 are each a separate component but AT3, AT4 and AT5 are grouped together as one (under the heading 'Writing').

Here are some examples of what is expected of children in the primary school.

Speaking and Listening for 5–7 year olds

LEVEL 1

- Participate as speakers and listeners in group activities, including imaginative play.

This could be practised in a story-telling session or when playing shopkeeper or customer in the class shop.

LEVEL 2

- Listen attentively to stories and poems, and talk about them.

Here, talking about the stories and poems is critical. For example, children should become accustomed to saying what they like or dislike about what they have heard. Active rather than passive listening is encouraged.

LEVEL 3

- Give, and receive and follow accurately, precise instructions when pursuing a task individually or as a member of a group.

This could involve planning a wall display or arranging an outing together.

When we move on to levels 8, 9 and 10, the range of difficulty across the National Curriculum is illustrated.

LEVEL 8

- Take an active part in group discussions, contributing constructively to the sustained development of the argument.

This might involve acting as the presenter in a television chat show, helping, for example, to sustain discussion.

LEVEL 9

- Show in discussion and in writing an awareness of the ways in which language varies between different types of spoken communication.

This could involve producing a guidebook for a foreign visitor, or composing different kinds of spoken language use such as jokes, anecdotes, conversation, commentary or lectures.

LEVEL 10

- Express a point of view on complex subjects persuasively, cogently and clearly, applying and interpreting a range of methods of presentation and assessing their own effectiveness accurately.

An activity which would allow this skill to be developed would be the devising and mounting of an advertising campaign concerned with a matter of principle.

You will see that most of these 'Speaking and writing' activities could be incorporated into lessons that also involve reading and writing (and spelling and handwriting). Some English classes might focus specifically on one attainment target, but the majority will cover a selection. Remember as well that at the primary school level especially, the subject matter may extend across a number of National Curriculum and other subjects.

Below are the type of attainments that eleven year-olds who have transferred to secondary school might be attempting. Imagine that the teacher had mounted an English project based around the pupils' personal interests or hobbies. Five relevant statements of attainment at level 6 would be:

AT1: Speaking and listening

- Use language to convey information and ideas effectively in a variety of situations where the subject is familiar to the pupils and the audience or other participants.

AT2: Reading

- Select from a range of reference materials, using appropriate methods to identify key points.

AT3: Writing

- Recognize when planning, that redrafting and revising are appropriate and act accordingly, either on paper or on a computer screen.

AT4/5: Presentation

- Check final drafts of writing for misspelling and other errors of presentation.
- Show some ability to use any available presentational devices that are appropriate to the task, so that finished work is presented clearly and attractively.

This selection, and there could have been many others, shows the potential for building the National Curriculum framework into imaginative and existing lesson plans. A few traditionalists saw the National Curriculum as a means of bringing back heavy emphasis on grammar-based English. In the event they were disappointed, as is illustrated clearly in the guidance given to teachers by the National Curriculum Council. Drama, for example, is seen as an important way of achieving the attainment targets in 'Speaking and listening'. This extract from the advice shows the range of activities that could be developed:

- play in a home-corner which is relevant to the work being pursued;
- group improvisation of a story (heard or read);
- puppet play;
- 'hot-seating' in which either the teacher or a member of the group adopts a role and is questioned by the rest of the class. In exploring a fictitious 'future world', for example, a child might agree to answer questions about the decisions made by the astronauts;
- 'forum theatre' in which a small group improvises the next stage in the drama, in order that the class can explore and discuss how a dilemma might be solved, for example during work on 'the circus', two children might show what happens when the RSPCA Inspector arrives to investigate a charge of cruelty to the elephants;
- 'teacher in role' in which the teacher plays a key part in shaping the direction of the drama, to make learning more effective. The teacher might take the role of the circus manager, who has discovered that the clown can no longer laugh, and ask for help and suggestions for resolving the problem;
- 'freeze frame' in which children in small groups devise a tableau which demonstrates what they want to say. The rest of the class is asked to interpret. The children might be asked to represent the relationship between the various members of the crew on the voyage to the 'future world';
- role-play and drama, for bilingual children, can be in two or more languages and can provide a very valuable way to enable children to use forms of language in English other than those already experienced.

These activities reflect the earlier views of the working party of experts that in 1988 began the task of devising the framework for English in the National Curriculum. They said that

> In the early stages, children need to explore their ideas through structured play or drama, through the use of apparatus and by drawing on their own experiences. In oral language work children interact with each other and with the teacher. This enables the teacher to build in new challenges, to suggest new ideas, and to give the children new experiences and new ways of thinking. Through this

kind of interaction children gain confidence in their own
ability as speakers. When they leave secondary school
much will depend on their ability to listen and to express
themselves clearly if they are to participate successfully
in adult life and work.

The debates that have surrounded the introduction of the
National Curriculum have helped clarify a number of issues. A
number of National Curriculum documents are critical of the
arguments that attempt to portray 'creative' and 'personal'
English as somehow in opposition to a 'grammar-based'
approach. The dichotomy is a false one. Clearly, English
contributes to the personal development of the child. Language
helps us to organize and make sense of experience. All of the
major national reports have commented on the significance of
language for intellectual, emotional and aesthetic development.
    The teaching of grammatically-sound spoken and written
English also has an important contribution to make to prepara-
tion for adult life. Everyone, as the National Curriculum English
experts said, needs to be able to communicate effectively and
appropriately in all the widely differing social situations in
which they find themselves. This means, amongst other things,
being able to write accurately and grammatically.
    There has also been considerable debate about how much
significance teachers should attach to the development of
Standard English. This is the phrase used to describe the type of
spoken English we hear from national television newsreaders.
Many teachers have argued that Standard English is not necessarily superior to other dialects, and that recognition must be
given to regional dialects and language variations such as West
Indian Creole. The experts who produced the working party
report on National Curriculum English were sympathetic to this
view. They recommended that all children should be entitled to
an English curriculum that teaches how to speak and write in
Standard English. It is, after all, the official national means of
communication and is important in many aspects of adult life.
But in doing this, they argued, the impression should not be
given that other dialects are somehow inferior.
    This illustrates an important feature of the way the National
Curriculum has been introduced. In the legal statutory documents on English, and in the guidance given to teachers by the
National Curriculum Council, the pros and cons of this argument
do not appear. There are frequent references to the importance

of the child understanding the use of language in different contexts. For example in the programme of study for English attainment target 1 (for infant classes) it is stipulated that all activities should:

> by informal and indirect means, develop pupils' ability to adjust the language they use and its delivery to suit particular audiences, purposes and contexts and, when listening to others, to respond to different ways of talking in different contexts and for different purposes. Pupils should therefore be encouraged to reflect on and evaluate their use of spoken language and to reformulate it to help the listener.

The official documentation tends to avoid politically controversial areas. The working party reports by experts are now mostly out of print and not all teachers received them. In schools, as a consequence, there may be different approaches to the issue of Standard English which parents and others will need to examine carefully. Not everyone, for example, will agree with placing regional dialects on a par with Standard English. One newspaper pundit was reduced to apoplexy!

Should do better

THAT education is far too important to leave to teachers and educationalists is shown once again in the final report on English in the national curriculum.

A group of eggheads led by Professor Brian Cox, Professor of English Literature at Manchester University, say that non-standard English like *we was*, *he ain't*, *she come here yesterday* and *they never saw nobody* should be treated as "objects of interest and value and not ridiculed".

The report says they are dialect forms, not errors, and "there is little point in correcting the spoken language of pupils in any general way because it is unlikely to have a beneficial effect against the pressures of home and peer group..."

So loons like Cox and his mob have sold the pass even before the first challenge!

For his information as a professor of English literature, *we was*, *he ain't*, *she come here yesterday* and *they never saw nobody* are not objects of interest and value.

Errors
They are not dialect, either. They are plain unarguable errors.

Children need to have them pointed out at as early an age as possible because if they go on using them they will be mocked and regarded as ill-educated, to say the least.

Indeed, children and the public in general should be protected as soon as possible against silly people like Cox and his mob.

One problem with this sort of argument is the assumption that Standard English is fixed and definable. Like all languages, it changes over time. It is also very complex, having developed through academic and administrative use in ways that other dialects could not. Even the most scrupulously drafted documents can fall victim to the intricate structure of rules. *The Times Educational Supplement* was quick to draw attention to a letter sent out by John MacGregor when he became Secretary of State for Education in succession to Kenneth Baker. In 1989 he wrote to all schools, and one paragraph was seen to contain nine errors! Try to spot them.

> 'I would like to take this first opportunity of writing direct to you to add my own personal thanks for the work that you and your staff do. I have already made clear on numerous occasions that I believe that the teaching profession deserve gratitude, recognition and respect for their professionalism and the commitment they show to their pupils.'

A further issue that the working party experts dealt with, but which the official documentation avoids, is the types of stories and literature that might be appropriate for use in schools. This, of course, is a very controversial issue. For example, the first working party report was criticized for not giving sufficient importance to the work of black authors. Great stress was placed, however, on the importance of reading in developing every child's educational potential. An official enquiry into the teaching of English in the 1980s (the Kingman enquiry) was quoted approvingly for saying:

We agree with the Kingman Report about the importance of the enjoyment of literature: 'From the earliest pre-school stages of development, children are interested in forms of language, such as the rhythms and rhymes of nursery tales, or the repetition of story structures. There is no doubt that all manner of linguistic artefacts, from the rebus of the primary class to the plays, poems, stories and essays of the 16 year old, have a tenacious grasp on the imagination of school age children. Wide reading, and as great an experience as possible of the best imaginative literature, are essential to the full development of an ear for language, and to a full knowledge of the range of possible patterns of thought and feeling made accessible by the power and range of language.'

The full list of authors is lengthy and extends to the writers of English textbooks for schools. Below are just twenty examples of the best known, recommended for primary age children.

1. Richard Adams
2. Louisa May Alcott
3. Rev. W. Awdry
4. Nina Bawden
5. Lewis Carroll
6. Roald Dahl
7. Anita Desai
8. Charles Dickens
9. Alan Garner
10. Roger Hargreaves
11. Ted Hughes
12. Erich Kastner
13. Ursula Le Guin
14. E. Nesbitt
15. Helen Oxenbury
16. Beatrix Potter
17. Rosemary Sutcliffe
18. J.R.R. Tolkien
19. Alison Utley
20. Jules Verne

Most people would be able to produce a comparable list, with twenty different authors designed to meet a variety of reading needs. Today, literature can be drawn from different countries and this provides an additional important source of general knowledge and awareness of the world at large.

Mathematics

In the 1960s, school mathematics across the world was swept by the *new maths* or *modern maths* revolution. The familiar sorts of sums and calculations disappeared and a new, rather bewildering terminology of sets, vectors and so forth was introduced.

The origins of this change lay in the developments that took place in university mathematics around the 1940s and 1950s. Many leading mathematicians argued that these changes in the higher education curriculum should be reflected in school mathematics. Their views were given added weight with the launch of the Russian Sputnik which seemed to imply that the West was lagging behind in technological development. As one *Sunday Times* newspaper commentator put it:

> It was, of course, the Russians who turned our maths classes into fun palaces. When Sputnik I circled Europe and America in 1957, its extraordinary wake smashed in one superior act the traditional mathematics which had dominated our schools unchallenged for a century. The maths that grandmother learnt was pretty hot at working out how many kippers at a penny-three-farthings each you might get for £5. But Greek geometry and Victorian mercantile conundrums clearly didn't lead to the stars.

New maths, however, was a short lived revolution. In a pure form it was never really implemented. By the 1970s most schools had adopted certain elements of it and rejected others.

By the time the National Curriculum came to be written, a degree of consensus had begun to emerge about what should be taught in schools. Inevitably, however, there were controversies. What was the place of mental arithmetic in the curriculum? Should calculators be allowed or not? What importance ought to be given to practical mathematics? Before examining the problems, we need to look at the framework for National Curriculum mathematics.

Mathematics has fourteen attainment targets. (In English there are only five. There is no significance in the difference. The groups of experts that prepared the frameworks worked separately and each made a subject-based decision on how many attainment targets were appropriate.)

The fourteen attainment targets in mathematics are:

AT1 –	Using and applying mathematics	Use number, algebra and measures in practical tasks, in real-life problems, and to investigate within mathematics itself.
AT2 –	Number	Understand number and number notation.
AT3 –	Number	Understand number operations (addition, subtraction, multiplication and division) and make use of appropriate methods of calculation.
AT4 –	Number	Estimate and approximate in number.

AT5 –	Number/ Algebra	Recognize and use patterns, relationships and sequences, and make generalizations.
AT6 –	Algebra	Recognize and use functions, formulae, equations and inequalities.
AT7 –	Algebra	Use graphical representation of algebraic functions.
AT8 –	Measures	Estimate and measure quantities, and appreciate the approximate nature of measurement.
AT9 –	Using and applying mathematics	Use shape and space and handle data in practical tasks, in real-life problems, and to investigate within mathematics itself.
AT10 –	Shape and space	Recognize and use the properties of two-dimensional and three-dimensional shapes.
AT11 –	Shape and space	Recognize location and use transformations in the study of space.
AT12 –	Handling data	Collect, record and process data.
AT13 –	Handling data	Represent and interpret data.
AT14 –	Handling data	Understand, estimate and calculate probabilities.

For reporting purposes there are two profile components: (i) attainment targets 1–8 – knowledge, skills, understanding and the use of number, algebra and measures; (ii) attainment targets 9–14 – knowledge, skills, understanding and the use of shape and space and data handling.

Here are some examples of what can be expected of children in the primary school. The statutory orders give examples against each statement of attainment to show how teaching plans could be developed.

Attainment target 5 is concerned with Number and Algebra. The aim is to develop the pupils' ability to recognize and use patterns, relationships and sequences and make generalizations.

LEVEL   STATEMENTS OF ATTAINMENT   EXAMPLE

Pupils should:

1 • Copy, continue and devise repeating patterns represented by objects/apparatus or one-digit numbers.   *Continue a threading bead pattern: red, red, blue, red, red, blue, . . .*
Continue the pattern 2,1,2,1,2,1, 2,1, . . .

2 • Explore and use the patterns in addition and subtraction facts to 10.

Use counters to make various combinations to given totals.

5 + 0 = 5	*5 = 4 + 1*
4 + 1 = 5	*= 3 + 2*
3 + 2 = 5	*= 3 + 1 + 1*
2 + 3 = 5	*= 2 + 2 + 1 etc.*
1 + 4 = 5	
0 + 5 = 5	

• Distinguish between odd and even numbers.

3 • Explain number patterns and predict subsequent numbers where appropriate.

Continue: 5, 10, 15, 20, . . .
Continue: 4 + 10 = 14,
14 + 10 = 24,
24 + 10 = 34, . . .

• Find number patterns and equivalent forms of 2-digit numbers and use these to perform mental calculations.

27 + 31 = 20 + 7 + 30 + 1
= 50 + 8
= 58.
35 + 29 = 35 + 30 − 1
= 65 − 1
= 64.

• Recognize whole numbers which are exactly divisible by 2, 5 and 10.

Levels 8, 9 and 10 illustrate the range of difficulty across this attainment target.

8 • Manipulate simple algebraic expressions.

Find common factors such as $a^2x + ax^2 = ax(a + x)$.

Transform formulae such as $V = IR$, $v = u + at$.

Multiply out two brackets $(ax + b)(cx + d)$.

• Solve a variety of linear and other inequalities.

Solve $3n + 4 < 17$, $x^2 \leqslant 16$.

• Understand and use a range of formulae and functions.

Use the formula $T = 2\pi\sqrt{1/g}$ to calculate one variable given the other.

9
- Express general laws in symbolic form.

  Work with direct proportion, inverse proportion and inverse square law.

- Use the rules of indices for negative and fractional values.

  Use $x^0 = 1$, $y^{-3} = \dfrac{1}{y^3}$, $\dfrac{x^2}{x^3} = \dfrac{1}{x} = x^{-1}$

  where neither x nor y is zero.

10
- Manipulate a range of algebraic expressions as needed in a variety of contexts.

  Factorize a variety of algebraic expressions.

  Solve quadratic equations by using factors, the common formula and iteration.

  Simplify $\dfrac{1}{x+2} + \dfrac{1}{x-3}$

  Show that
  $x^2 - 6x + 10 = (x-3)^2 + 1 \geqslant 1$,
  (whatever the value of x).

As in English, teachers will develop a range of topics that cover a number of attainment targets. The National Curriculum Council guidance describes two types of approach or teaching strategy. The first is where the teacher takes a theme or topic and, as it develops, monitors which parts of the National Curriculum are covered. A second approach is to focus on a specific area of attainment in the statutory orders. Most teachers will use a combination of these approaches. An example of the first strategy is given in the teachers' guidance notes. This could be for a class of eleven year-olds, and involves making a model with the largest possible surface area by linking six cubes together. Below are sample statements of attainment from six of the fourteen attainment targets. This topic could cover all of these.

AT1 LEVEL 5
- Select the materials and the mathematics to use for a task; check there is sufficient information; work methodically and review progress.

AT2 LEVEL 4
- Read, write and order whole numbers.

AT3 LEVEL 4

- Know multiplication facts up to 10 x 10 and use them in multiplication and division problems.
- (Using whole numbers) add or subtract mentally two 2-digit numbers; add mentally several single-digit numbers; without a calculator add and subtract two 3-digit numbers, multiplying a 2-digit number by a single digit number and divide a 2-digit number by a single digit number.

AT5 LEVEL 5

- Understand and use terms such as prime, square, cube, square root, cube root, multiples and factors.
- Recognize patterns in numbers through spatial arrangements.

LEVEL 6

- Determine possible rules for generating a sequence.
- Use spreadsheets or other computer facilities to explore number patterns.

LEVEL 7

- Use symbolic notation to express the rules of sequences (mainly linear and quadratic).
- Understand the meaning of reciprocals and explore relationships.

LEVEL 8

- Understand the role of a counter-example in the context of rules for sequences and in disproving hypotheses.

AT6 LEVEL 5

- Express a simple function symbolically.

There are also statements of attainment in AT8 'Measures' and AT10 'Shape and space' that are relevant – these are marked with an asterisk on the chart below.

| 4 | • Understand and use language associated with angles. | *Know acute, obtuse and reflex angles, parallel, perpendicular, vertical and horizontal, etc.* |
| | * • Construct simple 2-D and 3-D shapes from given information and know associated language. | *Construct triangles, rectangles, circles, nets for cubes, pyramids and prisms.* |

5   * • Understand congruence
        of simple shapes.

        *Group together congruent
        shapes from a range of shapes.*

     • Explain and use angle
       properties associated
       with intersecting and
       parallel lines and
       triangles, and know
       associated language.

       *Identify equal angles in a
       diagram.*

6   • Know and use angle
       properties and symmetry
       properties of quadri-
       laterals and other poly-
       gons.

       *Determine whether a
       tessellation of given
       shapes is possible.*

     * • Recognize and use
         common 2-D represen-
         tation of 3-D objects.

       *Use isometric paper to
       represent 3-D.*

       *Read simple plans and
       elevations.*

     • Use computers to
       generate and transform
       2-D shapes.

       *Use LOGO to draw regular
       polygons and other shapes.*

     • Classify and define types
       of quadrilaterals.

The examples selected range across a number of levels. Many lessons will deal with a variety of attainment targets, and they will also cover more than one level of attainment. This reflects the way the good teacher has always worked. For example, pupils normally working at levels 5 and 6 may need to revise some skills or concepts covered at level 3 or 4. If the children are working individually on a topic, some may be studying up to level 8 in certain aspects of it. The attainment targets and statements of attainment are not meant 'to produce a narrow or mechanistic approach to learning or teaching mathematics, through a rigid interpretation of the systems of levels within the programmes of study'. This quotation is taken from the guidance given to teachers of mathematics by the National Curriculum Council.

The National Curriculum in mathematics has reinforced a number of trends that were already underway. For example, on the issue of calculators and mental arithmetic, the expert group that set down the mathematics framework gave a clear view that a variety of methods were appropriate.

There is no doubt that the role of calculators and computers in the mathematics classroom excites a great deal of public interest – not least because of the debate about 'pencil and paper' versus 'calculator' methods and concern about the decline of 'mental arithmetic' skills. At times it has appeared as if these approaches were somehow mutually exclusive.

The calculator can and is doing for us what the water-frame and the spinning jenny did for the textile industry in the last century – reducing drudgery and greatly increasing the potential for both output and quality. There is no 'moral gain' derived from tackling 1000 long divisions when calculators exist; on the other hand the time saved can be used to improve standards of attainment. That is the goal our report sets – the harnessing of technology to enhance achievement at every stage of schooling, and beyond.

To enter the world of work young people need skills appropriate to today's needs. As we have already noted in this chapter, the old repetitive drudgery carried out by clerks on high stools with quill pens has long been replaced by applied mathematics and technological know-how. Commercial and administrative routines are now dependent on calculators, computers and word processors for their speed, accuracy – and profitability.

It is understandable that many people are concerned about the effect of the calculator on standards. If pupils are able to get the right answer to all their sums at the press of a button, why should they bother to learn to do the sums for themselves, unaided by electronics? Are we at risk of producing a generation of school leavers entirely dependent on their calculators, with no knowledge and understanding of what is involved in the number functions which calculators are programmed to perform? These are serious questions, about which people are right to seek reassurance. it is, however, absurd to ignore calculators – to pretend that they do not exist and have not transformed the way mathematics is applied in the world outside school.

The challenge is to teach children to use calculators effectively.

Many people who express concern about calculators believe that the more traditional methods of calculation – particularly pencil and paper methods – were in themselves a guarantee of high standards of attainment. We do not accept this premise. The key to effective use of any method of calculation, be it mental, pencil and paper, or electronic, is a knowledge of and feel for number itself. It is this which is the essential basic skill, not the methods of calculation. Fluency in appropriate methods of calculation, though it is a necessary skill, is not sufficient.

The reality is that at different levels and in different contexts, we need to use different methods of calculation – mental, pencil and paper and electronic. The electronic calculator has extended the range of methods available, but some of the time honoured methods are still needed. Our aim should be to equip children with a range of methods for doing calculations and with the ability to use them effectively and appropriately in different situations.

The message is very clear. As in English teaching, the approach will depend on the end to which the pupil is working. Learning about the variety of methods and purposes is part of the mathematics curriculum, and the use of calculators, computers and mental reasoning are all built into the programme of study and attainment targets.

The National Curriculum also aims to make applied and practical mathematics an important part of the subject. This is shown in a number of ways. Firstly the examples of activities include a goodly number that allow the teacher to organize visits out of schools, organize group work and generally make the issues studied relevant to the pupils' interests. Attainment target 13 'Handling data' at level 6 shows how a variety of imaginative activities could be developed.

LEVEL	STATEMENTS OF ATTAINMENT Pupils should	EXAMPLE

6
- Create scatter graphs for discrete and continuous variables and have a basic understanding of correlation.

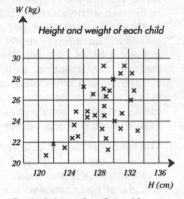

Height and weight of each child

- Construct, describe and interpret information through two-way tables.

Record the orders from 10 people for various alternatives in a restaurant.

- Construct and interpret network diagrams which represent relationships or connections.

Use network diagrams to represent railway/airline connections between a number of major cities.

Another aspect of practical and applied mathematics is the extent to which the curriculum prepares young people for the mathematics they will need at work. This is another area of controversy. Over the years, employers have been quick to criticize the mathematical achievements of school leavers. The expert mathematics group writing the National Curriculum was asked to look at standards in general, and the relevance to working life in particular. In Section 2 the standards debate was explored in some detail. The problems of making historical comparisons (for example whether pupils' achievements at certain ages declined in the 1960s and 1970s) and international comparisons (do French or Japanese pupils achieve more highly than English and Welsh pupils of the same age?) was considered in some detail in the mathematics report. As in most analyses, a clear conclusion about whether standards had fallen or not proved impossible. What the experts did say was that evidence existed to show that pupils in this country ought to be, and were capable of, aiming for much higher standards. The following chart shows examples of test questions set to thirteen year-olds, to illustrate the concern about the large proportion of children who did not appear competent in certain basic skills.

For example:

Questions (an asterisk indicates the correct response)	% of pupils responding (England and Wales)
a) The arithmetic average of: 1·50, 2·40, 3·75 is equal to	1981
A 2·40	10
B 2·55*	36
C 3·75	4
D 7·65	31
E None of these	14

b)

On the above scale the reading
indicated by the arrow is between

A 51 and 52	2
B 57 and 58	33
C 60 and 62	3
D 62 and 64	19
E 64 and 66*	43

c) The value of $2^3 \times 3^2$ is

A 30	6
B 36	27
C 64	5
D 72*	35
E None of these	25

A more significant issue than standards is the type of mathematics used in work. Surveys have shown that just about every job requires use of one or more of the arithmetical operations. As the National Curriculum mathematics working group said, reading recall of number bonds (for example, $10 = 9 + 1 = 8 + 2 = 7 + 3...$) and multiplication tables is also important in a wide range of jobs. They also found that it is extremely rare to find employees using the longer written processes for arithmetical calculations. Written calculations with fractions are now rare, and calculators and computers are used extensively. Given the changes in technology the interpretation, rather than the assembly of data is of great importance. Hence the emphasis on handling data in the National Curriculum.

The vocational significance of mathematics is recognized in the framework. Mathematics, however, should also be seen as enjoyable in its own right. There are numerous references to this in National Curriculum documentation, and the examples in the statutory orders show how imaginatively the framework could be applied in schools. A critical aspect of the child's success in mathematics is the confidence and attitudes brought to the subject. Parents and other adults have a crucial role here. If they give the impression that somehow 'maths is difficult' or that it was a subject they 'never enjoyed at school', then negative associations will be established. In reading and writing, parental involvement from the earliest age helps the child's development inside and outside school. All the evidence shows that the same is true of mathematics.

Science

Introducing changes in the school curriculum is far from easy. All sorts of vested interests amongst teachers, parents and the public at large can be threatened. Some research in the 1980s showed how the pupils themselves can prove resistant to innovation. In many ways this is a healthy reaction. The education system is susceptible to fads and fancies, and a degree of healthy scepticism is often warranted. It is, however, strange that only in the 1990s has the teaching of science become a priority issue in both primary and secondary schools. From the 1960s onwards scientists, science teachers and industrialists have argued strongly for science curriculum reform. Even the Royal Society gave prestigious support to the need for change. In Section 2 the patchy, even non-existent provision in primary schools was commented on. At secondary level, the divisions into physics, chemistry and biology have meant that significant issues such as earth sciences or astronomy have been ignored. At the age of fourteen some pupils dropped science completely, and others may have opted to continue the study of just one subject. Many boys chose physics and ignored biology. For girls it was the reverse. The National Curriculum plans for science aim to put an end to these inconsistencies. School science may continue to be taught by specialists, especially at secondary level, but every pupil is now entitled to a balanced science curriculum, covering all the major scientific disciplines.

The statutory orders in science describe seventeen attainment targets for pupils. There are two profile components, the first relating only to attainment target 1, and the second covering the additional sixteen attainment targets.

Profile component	Exploration of science, communication and the application of knowledge and understanding
AT1	Exploration of science
Profile component	Knowledge and understanding of science, communication, and the applications and implications of science
AT2	The variety of life
AT3	Processes of life
AT4	Genetics and evolution
AT5	Human influences on the Earth
AT6	Types and uses of materials
AT7	Making new materials
AT8	Explaining how materials behave
AT9	Earth and atmosphere
AT10	Forces
AT11	Electricity and magnetism
AT12	The scientific aspects of information technology including microelectronics
AT13	Energy
AT14	Sound and music
AT15	Using light and electromagnetic radiation
AT16	The Earth in space
AT17	The nature of science

This is called Model A.

There is a second, modified version of the National Curriculum in science, termed Model B. Pupils, in consultation with teachers and parents, can opt for either Model A or Model B in the final stage of secondary schooling at key stage 4. Model B is a more restricted programme that can be studied in less time. As a rule of thumb, Model A assumes the study of science for 20 per cent of the school's weekly timetable, Model B for 12.5 per cent.

Model B

Profile component		Exploration of science, communication and the application of knowledge and understanding
	AT1	Exploration of science
Profile component		Knowledge and understanding of science, communication, and the applications and implications of science
	AT3	Processes of life
	AT4	Genetics and evolution
	AT6	Types and uses of materials
	AT8	Explaining how materials behave
	AT9	Earth and atmosphere
	AT10	Forces
	AT11	Electricity and magnetism
	AT13	Energy
	AT14	Sound and music

The diagram below shows how the attainment targets are planned in relation to key stages.

Key stage 1: supports ATs 1–6 and 9–16; levels 1–3
Key stage 2: supports ATs 1–6, and 9–16; levels 2–5
Key stage 3: supports ATs 1–17; levels 3–7
Key stage 4: (Model A): supports ATs 1–17; levels 4–10
Key stage 4: (Model B): supports ATs 1, 3–4, 6, 8–11, 13–14; levels 4–10

There has been considerable controversy about the Model A–Model B approach, with the majority of science education experts arguing that all key stage 4 children should experience the full (Model A) programme. This is an area where modifications may occur, particularly when the relationship of the science statutory orders to GCSE is determined. Schools, and science teachers in particular, will be able to provide more detailed information when key stage 4 teaching programmes are implemented.

Examples of what can be expected of children in the primary school are set out below. Two examples are given for attainment target 1, 'Explorations of science' and attainment target 3, 'Processes of Life'. Both these attainment targets are covered in Models A and B.

Attainment target 1: Exploration of science

LEVEL STATEMENTS OF ATTAINMENT

Pupils should:

1
  - Observe familiar materials and events in their immediate environment, at first hand, using their senses.
  - Describe and communicate their observations, ideally through talking in groups or by other means, within their class.

2
  - Ask questions and suggest ideas of the 'how', 'why', and 'what will happen if' variety.
  - Identify simple differences, for example, *hot/cold, rough/smooth.*
  - Use non-standard and standard measures, for example, *hand-spans and rulers.*
  - List and collate observations.
  - Interpret findings by associating one factor with another, for example, *the pupils' perception at this level that 'light objects float', 'thin wood is bendy'.*
  - Record findings in charts, drawings and other appropriate forms.

3
  - Formulate hypotheses, for example, *'this ball will bounce higher than that one'.*
  - Identify and describe simple variables that change over time, for example, *growth of a plant.*
  - Distinguish between a 'fair' and an 'unfair' test.
  - Select and use simple instruments to enhance observations, for example, *a stop-clock or hand lens.*
  - Quantify variables, as appropriate, to the nearest labelled division of simple measuring instruments, for example, *a rule.*
  - Record experimental findings, for example, *in tables and bar charts.*
  - Interpret simple pictograms and bar charts.
  - Interpret observations in terms of a generalized statement, for example, *the greater the suspended weight, the longer the spring.*
  - Describe activities carried out by sequencing the major features.

Attainment Target 3: Processes of life

LEVEL   STATEMENTS OF ATTAINMENT

Pupils should:

1   • Be able to name or label the external parts of the human body/plants, for example, *arm, leg/flower, stem.*

2   • Know that living things reproduce their own kind.
     • Know that personal hygiene, food, exercise, rest and safety, and the proper and safe use of medicines are important.
     • Be able to give a simple account of the pattern of their own day.

3   • Know that the basic life processes: feeding, breathing, movement and behaviour, are common to human beings and the other living things they have studied.
     • Be able to describe the main stages in the human life cycle.

Higher-attaining secondary pupils in the same attainment targets will be expected to attempt the sort of work set out at levels 8, 9 and 10.

Attainment Target 1: Exploration of science

8   • Be able to perform an experiment to elucidate a theory, concept or model, and use the results to demonstrate a clear understanding of the ideas that led to that theory, concept or model.
     • Make generalizations from several data sets including self-generated data.
     • Prepare and deliver a report matched to audience which incorporates background material from a variety of sources.

9   • In the context of an extended investigation:
       • Initiate a piece of self-generated background research employing a variety of sources of information.
       • Plan a range of exploratory techniques, for example, *experiments, literature searches, data logging and analysis.*
       • Interpret data in the light of experimental findings and appropriate scientific knowledge and understanding.
       • Draw conclusions and make inferences using, as appropriate, data tables and statistical data.
       • Make a presentation of their research and investigation.

10 • In the context of the investigation defined in level 9, be able to:
- • Evaluate critically the entire project in terms of sources of unreliability and invalidity.
- • Suggest alternative and considered improvements to experimental technique.
- • Formulate further testable hypotheses supported by the knowledge and understanding generated.

Attainment Target 3: Processes of life

8 • Be able to describe how the functions of the major organ systems contribute to maintaining the internal environment in plants, animals and human embryos.
- • Understand that infective organisms and drugs can disrupt the normal functioning of the body and how the body's natural defences may be enhanced by immunization and the use of medicines.
- • Be able to give a basic explanation and evaluation of the impact of life supporting technology, for example, *incubators, pacemakers and kidney machines*, in improving and sustaining the quality of life.

9 • Understand how environmental factors can be varied to enhance photosynthesis.
- • Be able to make informed judgements about the benefits and drawbacks underlying the use of hormones and growth regulators in controlling growth, development and fertility in plants and animals.

10 • Understand how homeostatic and metabolic processes contribute to maintaining the internal environment of organisms.

There are numerous justifications for the teaching of science to all pupils. The expert group that came up with the recommendations for the balanced programme provided an eloquent statement that has been used in part by the National Curriculum Council in writing guidance for primary and secondary science teachers.

The contribution of Science to the school curriculum

Schools have an important role to play in helping children to understand the world they live in, and in preparing them for adult life and work. We are mindful of the value of our task in helping to equip these citizens of the next century with an education which should stand them in good stead in a world that will be very different from our own. We believe that science has an essential contribution to make in the following ways:

i. Understanding scientific ideas

Scientists have developed a powerful body of knowledge about physical and biological phenomena. Science education should provide opportunities for all pupils to develop an understanding of key concepts and enable them to be used in unfamiliar situations. To allow this to happen, pupils need to understand and explore their use in a range of contexts; the study of pure or formal science by itself can lead to ineffective learning by many pupils. Technological applications, personal health or the environment can often provide contexts through which scientific concepts can be more effectively introduced and developed.

ii. Developing scientific methods of investigation

All pupils should be enabled to learn and to use scientific methods of investigation. They should have the opportunity to develop the skills of imaginative but disciplined enquiry which include systematic observation, making and testing hypotheses, designing and carrying out experiments competently and safely, drawing inferences from evidence, formulating and communicating conclusions in an appropriate form and applying them to new situations. Pupils should come to learn how to gain access to, and use selectively and appropriately, published scientific knowledge.

iii. Relating science to other areas of knowledge

Just as science cannot offer an adequate explanation of our world on its own, so science education needs to relate to other areas of the school curriculum. Pupils should be encouraged to recognize and value the contribution which science can make to other areas of learning, and the knowledge, skills and inspiration which scientists can derive from other activities.

iv. Understanding the contribution science makes to society

Pupils should be encouraged to study the practical applications of science and technology and the ways they are changing the nature of our society and our economy. They should be helped to explore some of the moral dilemmas that scientific discoveries and technological developments can cause. Science education should encourage all pupils to appreciate their responsibilities as members of society and give them the confidence to make a positive contribution to it.

v. Recognising the contribution science education makes to personal development

Productive learning needs the right conditions. Successful science and technology education requires pupils to combine interest and curiosity with a responsible attitude towards safety and a respect for living organisms and the physical environment. It should help to develop other attitudes such as a willingness to accept uncertainty, to co-operate with others, to give honest reports and to think critically. A study of science is an important dimension of health education and pupils should become aware of its relevance to matters of personal and public health. Understanding and clarifying one's own thinking is often an essential part of learning. Throughout their science education, pupils should be encouraged to develop their powers of reasoning by reflecting on their own understanding, and by appreciating that learning may involve a change in the way they think about, explain and do things.

vi. Appreciating the nature of scientific knowledge

Pupils should further their understanding of science by exploring the social and historical contexts of scientific discoveries. Through this they can begin to

appreciate the powerful but provisional nature of
scientific explanation, and the process by which
models are created, tested and modified in the light
of evidence. Most important of all, they will be
reminded of the excitement of discovery that has
been the continual inspiration of all scientists.

Recent developments in our understanding of the way children
learn have been incorporated into the programmes and advice
for the teaching of science. For example, practical investigative
approaches are given a prominent place through the first attainment target which is also a profile component. This will be given
a heavier emphasis in overall assessments than any other
attainment target. Investigative abilities are seen to develop as
the children mature and as they are brought into contact with
new contexts and areas of knowledge. Skills of investigation and
knowledge of the attainment targets are seen to develop alongside positive attitudes towards the subject. A lively and imaginative science programme can help children develop the
following:

- curiosity
- respect for evidence
- willingness to tolerate uncertainty
- critical reflection
- perseverance
- creativity and inventiveness
- open-mindedness
- sensitivity to the living and non-living environment
- co-operation with others.

A parent who went to school in the 1950s, 1960s, or even 1970s
would probably find that science is the subject in which there
has been the most significant change. Experiments and investigations should now feature in most lessons. The situation where
the teacher demonstrates an experiment which the pupils then
try to copy exactly will be very rare. Experimentation is much
more open-ended than it used to be.

The National Curriculum Council's non-statutory (not legally
binding) guidance to teachers describes a primary school
where the staff have planned the science curriculum around a
chart.

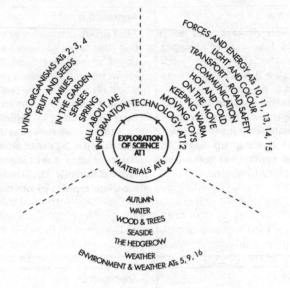

Each class teacher chooses two segments from the chart each year. A record is kept to avoid repetition, and this is built into the school's record-keeping system. A teacher might plan a year's work in the following way:

Autumn term	Fruits and seeds
	Moving toys
Spring term	Water
	Senses
Summer term	Light and colour
	Seaside

Part of the 'Moving toys' topic includes an investigation which looks at how windmills work. Following class discussion of a toy windmill, the children are divided into groups to make a model windmill. The National Curriculum Council describes four different ways in which the teacher could organize the groups.

Approach A

Discussion of task and why tackle it. Take a sheet of paper cut to the right size with marking on it and instructions on what to do with it – cut, fold, stick, make hole, attach, etc. Explore how to make it rotate (near heater, running in the playground, holding up high in windiest spot). Oral communication, picture painting.

Approach B

After group discussion of task and the variety of papers which could be used, decide which might be used to make a paper windmill similar to the real one; use of a template to cut and then make (using example). Try to rotate in different situations, compare findings with others, consider what makes them move differently. Oral communication, simple tick chart.

Approach C

The group discuss and consider how they might make a paper windmill (no example given), with stimulus of range of materials, including paper cups for example, with opportunity then to try out own ideas, make, modify, remake, gather the resulting models, test in similar ways and compare. Collate and record results in appropriate ways.

Approach D

Making a windmill according to an agreed format, after initial stage of exploration. Identification of variables that may effect the efficiency of the windmill, e.g. size of paper, type of material, number of vanes, means of attaching to rod, etc. Groups to select and test one variable, combine results at end. Display results graphically, interpret findings, make a generalised statement. Choose the best material, number of vanes, etc., to make a 'super windmill'.

At the primary level, the teacher will also be thinking about simultaneous development towards attainment targets in English and mathematics. There are clearly important links with technology as well.

At the secondary level, science will almost always be taught as a separate subject with specialist laboratories available. Attainment target 1, 'Exploration of science', will be central to the curriculum although most lessons and activities will incorporate one or more additional attainment targets.

The advice given to teachers by the National Curriculum Council offers a number of examples of how this can be achieved.

> Pupils could be set a task on house insulation. This would involve them in looking at their own house, and testing materials to see which provides the best insulation. At the end of the project they could write a report to their parents on how to economize on energy!

The pupil would be developing competence at level 6 of Attainment target 1.

6 • contribute to the analysis and investigation of a collaborative exercise in which outcomes are derived from the results of a number of different lines of enquiry, possibly including experimentation, survey and use of secondary sources, in the context of which each pupil should:
  • Use experience and knowledge to make predictions in new contexts.
  • Identify and manipulate two discrete independent variables and control other variables.
  • Prepare a detailed written plan, where the key variables are named and details of the experiment procedure are given.
  • Record data in tables and translate it into appropriate graphical forms.
  • Produce reports which include a critical evaluation of certain features of the experiment, such as reliability, validity of measurements and experimental design.

They would also be covering parts of Attainment target 13, 'Energy', across levels 5, 6 and 7.

5 • Understand the need for fuel economy and efficiency.
  • Understand the idea of global energy resources and appreciate that these resources are limited.

6 • Be able to recognize different types of energy source and follow some processes of energy transfer in terms of the principle of conservation of energy.
  • Understand that energy is conserved, but becomes spread around and so is less useful.

- Be able to explain the distinctive features which make machines, such as pulleys and levers, useful in everyday life.
- Understand that the Sun is ultimately the major energy source for the Earth.

7
- Understand energy transfer by conduction, convection and radiation in solids, liquids and gases and the methods of controlling these transfers, particularly of insulation in domestic and everyday contexts.
- Know that efficiency is a measure of how much energy is transferred in an intended way.
- Be able to evaluate the methods used to reduce energy consumption in the home.

A further example is an investigation to find out how light and temperature affect the growth rate of trees. The pupils here could be working at level 7 of attainment target 1. At this level, they are expected to be able to identify and manipulate two independent variables. They will be looking at how many different temperatures and how many different intensities of light are sufficient to give a solution. The task, therefore, is to design and carry out an investigation. Attainment targets 2 and 3, 'The variety of life' and 'Processes of life', will be covered in this topic.

A final example, at a more advanced level, is in the area of kinetic theory. Pupils could look at the alternative merits of different forms of protection against corrosion (for example, points, electrolytic coatings, galvanizing). The sort of skills that could be developed at levels 8, 9 and 10 are given on pages 56–57 (AT1 'Exploration of science'). Two extracts from attainment target 6 and attainment target 8 show the knowledge targets that would be included in the teacher's plans.

AT6: Types of uses of material

9
- Be able to describe simple trends in properties of a group of metals and of non-metals, within the periodic table, and relate these to their electronic structure.
- Be able to collect and use quantitative measurements of properties of materials, including cost, to make judgements about the use of different materials.

10
- Understand the construction of the periodic table in terms of atomic structure for important elements.

- Understand the limitations of systems of classification.
- Be able to evaluate the relative advantages of composite materials.
- Be able to use scientific knowledge and information from a range of sources to evaluate the social, economic, health and safety and environmental factors associated with manufacturing a metal or a ceramic or a plastic or a fibre.

AT8: Explaining how materials behave

9
- Be able to interpret chemical equations quantitatively.
- Know that there are different types of ionising radiations, each with different properties.
- Be able to give a coherent account of the properties of different types of ionising radiation.
- Be able to explain the meaning of half-life.

10
- Be able to apply the kinetic theory in a range of contexts.
- Be able to explain electrolysis in terms of ionic reactions.
- Be able to relate the bulk properties of metals, ceramics, glass, plastics and fibres to simple models of their structures.
- understand the relationship between the half-life and the nature of the radioactive source, in the use of radioactive materials.

The foundation subjects
of the National Curriculum:

technology, history, geography, modern languages, art, music and physical education

Most of the foundation subjects are defined in the same way as the core foundation subjects described in Section 5. Working parties were set up to decide on programmes of study, attainment targets and the statements of attainment that apply at each of the ten levels, and the profile components. In music, art and physical education it is likely that the statutory orders will be less detailed, and therefore less prescriptive, than in technology, history, geography and modern languages.

Technology

The introduction of technology into the primary and secondary curriculum is one of the major innovations of the National Curriculum. For some time a growing body of opinion had been arguing for technology to be given far greater importance at all levels of schooling. This was acknowledged in the first consultation document on the National Curriculum, and the technology working party was the first to be set up after the core foundation subject groups. The final report it produced was one of the least controversial, perhaps in part because so few people had had direct experience of the subject in their own school days.

The National Curriculum Council, in the foreword of the document that made the final recommendations to the Secretary of State, underlined why every child should study technology:

> Technology is the one subject in the National Curriculum that is directly concerned with generating ideas, making and doing. In emphasising the importance of practical capability, and providing opportunities for pupils to develop their powers to innovate, to make decisions, to create new solutions, it can play a unique role. Central to this role is the task of providing balance in a curriculum based on academic subjects – a balance in which the creative and practical capabilities of pupils can be fully developed and interrelated. The subject has a crucial part to play in helping pupils

to develop these important personal qualities and competencies.

Whilst the contribution of technology to the personal development of individuals is very important, of equal importance is its role in helping pupils to respond to the employment needs of business and industry. Pupils will become aware of technological developments and the way in which technology is changing the work place and influencing life styles. They will learn that technological change cannot be reversed and will understand Its enormous power. Knowledge of technology enables citizens to be prepared to meet the needs of the 21st century and to cope with a rapidly changing society.

This dual justification, for personal development and in developing an awareness of the needs of business and industry, is reflected in the programmes of study and the attainment targets.

There are five attainment targets. The first four are grouped together as one profile component for reporting to parents.

Profile component: Design and technology capability

AT1: Identifying needs and opportunities

Pupils should be able to identify and state clearly needs and opportunities for design and technological activities through investigation of the contexts of home, school, recreation, community, business and industry.

AT2: Generating a design

Pupils should be able to generate a design specification, explore ideas to produce a design proposal and develop it into a realistic, appropriate and achievable design.

AT3: Planning and making

Pupils should be able to make artefacts, systems and environments, preparing and working to a plan and identifying, managing and using appropriate resources, including knowledge and processes.

AT4: Evaluating

Pupils should be able to develop, communicate and act upon an evaluation of the process, products and effects of their design and technological activities and of those of others, including those from other times and cultures.

The fifth attainment target corresponds to the second profile component.

Profile component: Information technology capability

AT5: Information technology capability

Pupils should be able to use information technology to:

* communicate and handle information;
* design, develop, explore and evaluate models of real or imaginary situations;
* measure and control physical variables and movement.

They should be able to make informed judgements about the application and importance of information technology, and its effect on the quality of life.

Within the technology attainment targets, information technology capability is given a specific place (attainment target 5). As many National Curriculum documents make clear, information technology (IT) plays a part in the teaching of most subjects. In technology, however, it has a central role and therefore merits a separate attainment target.

The diagram below shows how the attainment targets are planned to relate to key stages.

SPECIFICATION OF ATTAINMENT TARGETS

(1) *Key stages*	(2) *Attainment targets*
First key stage	Attainment targets 1–5; levels 1–3
Second key stage	Attainment targets 1–5; levels 2–5
Third key stage	Attainment targets 1–5; levels 3–7
Fourth key stage	Attainment targets 1–5; levels 4–10

Examples of what can be expected of children in the primary school from attainment targets 2 and 3 are set out below.

> Pupils should be able to generate a design specification, explore ideas to produce a design proposal and develop it into a realistic, appropriate and achievable design.

LEVEL	STATEMENTS OF ATTAINMENT	EXAMPLES
	Pupils should be able to:	
1	• Express their ideas about what they might do to meet an identified need or opportunity.	*Draw pictures showing different ways of scaring birds in a field of crops.*
2	• Use talk, pictures, drawings, models, to develop their design proposals, giving simple reasons why they have chosen to make their design.	*Explain why they have chosen to make bird scarers. Draw a picture showing how they will make a scarecrow and say how it will scare away the birds from crops.*
3	• Make a design proposal by selecting from their ideas and giving reasons for their choices.	*Explain why they have chosen certain features of their different designs for a desk tidy to use in their design proposal.*
	• Apply knowledge and skills to select ideas for different parts of their design.	*Choose from a range of designs and materials, produced by their class for the front cover and contents of a class book on pets.*
	• Draw from information about materials, people, markets and processes and from other times and cultures to help in developing their ideas.	*Gather information on different types of ethnic food and people's preferences when planning a party.*
	• Use models including annotated drawings and three-dimensional working models to develop their design.	*Use a model, drawing, or an existing example, to try out different ideas for the detail of a bird scarer.*

- Record how they have explored different ideas about a design and technological proposal to see how realistic it might be.

Record different designs for bird scarers, a rattle, a kite.

Pupils should be able to make artefacts, systems and environments, preparing and working to a plan and identifying, managing and using appropriate resources, including knowledge and processes.

LEVEL	STATEMENTS OF ATTAINMENT	EXAMPLES
	Pupils should be able to:	
1	• Use a variety of materials and equipment to make simple things.	*Use scissors, paper and paint to make a decorative protection for a display table.*
2	• Describe to others how they are going about their work.	*Describe their actions to their group or to a visitor.*
	• Use knowledge of the working characteristics of materials and components, including construction kits, in making artefacts, systems or environments.	*When building a model roundabout use sandpaper to smooth wood, allow enough time for the paint to dry.*
	• Show that they can use simple hand tools, materials and components.	*Use tools for cutting and shaping clay to make a model.*
3	• Consider constraints of time and availability of resources in planning and making.	
	• Choose resources for making by using their knowledge of the characteristics of materials and components.	*Where glue is used in making a mobile, choose a type appropriate to the materials used.*

- Use a range of hand tools and equipment, appropriate to the materials and components, with some regard for accuracy and quality.

  Choose an appropriate tool to drill, cut, smooth and join different materials such as wood, clay, paper, card, fabric, polystyrene to make a boat.

- Improvise within the limits of materials, resources and skills when faced with unforeseen difficulties.

  When a glue will not stick a model together recognize that alternative methods might work instead e.g. another glue, staples, Sellotape.

High-attaining secondary pupils, in the same attainment targets, will be expected to attempt the work set out at levels 8, 9, 10.

8
- Record and present, using a range of methods and media, the progress of their ideas; detail and refine their design proposal and incorporate modifications; use computer aided design, image generation and desk top publishing techniques, where appropriate, to explore, detail and refine their ideas.

  Present interim ideas for a school magazine, using mock-ups and scale drawings and use audience feedback to refine the design using computer supported editing techniques.

- Plan their activities to take into account multiple constraints which may at times be conflicting.

  Make a plan for a piece of jewellery within a fixed budget. Match the size and complexity of the piece with the cost of the material and the time required to make it.

- Show a willingness, subject to safety considerations, to experiment and take risks recognizing the implications of decisions taken in designing.

  Produce a design proposal for an experimental new food product. Explore ideas involving novel uses of common materials (cf. concrete in boatbuilding).

9

- Develop ideas by drawing on information and understanding from a broad knowledge of sources, and showing judgement about the detail required.

  Bringing together the best parts of different ideas after further research. How could the design be improved? What problems are still likely to exist and how could the design be changed to overcome these? Know when they have enough information of sufficient accuracy for the next stage of development of their design proposal.

- Refine their design to achieve an optimum practicable outcome demonstrating originality and understanding of constraints in the justification of their design.

  Develop a series of linked spreadsheets to be used by a builder to calculate the cost of building home extensions.

10

- Provide a substantiated account of the full range of ideas they have explored and the strategies used showing:
  (i) How they explored ideas used in existing artefacts, systems or environments and how they used them to develop their own ideas;
  (ii) Evidence that they have:
  - identified ways of improving and refining their proposals;
  - predicted with accuracy the outcomes of possible improvements and refinements;
  - resolved conflicting demands;
  - included their decisions in a coherent specification;

  Through a presentation and exhibition, which includes a comprehensive folio of drawings, sketches, models, technical drawing and other techniques, show evidence of thorough investigation of existing artefacts, systems and environments and how and why they incorporated some features of these and rejected others. It will also contain evidence of thorough research of needs and opportunities, original ideas and a justification of all decisions taken in refining their proposal including fitness for purpose, experiments, tests and trials.

and using an appro-
priate range of
media and methods.

Note: Pupils unable to communicate by speech, writing or drawing may use other means including the use of technology or symbols as alternatives.

LEVEL	STATEMENTS OF ATTAINMENT	EXAMPLES
8	• Review how to make best use of materials, procedures, tools and equipment.	*Experiment with alternative techniques in order to simplify or improve the methods of realization of a design.*
	• Show evidence of knowledge of making processes and devise and implement proced-ures for quality assurance.	*Develop quality assurance features within the planned production at key points, for example in silk screen printing.*
	• Identify and incorporate modifications during making.	*Solve the problem of a blind spot on an infra-red detector by modifying position of a sensor, introducing another type of sensor or increasing sensitivity.*
9	• Make judgements about the quality and usefulness of sources of advice and information consulted during planning and making.	
	• Demonstrate how they have overcome constraints encountered in planning and making to achieve a quality product.	
	• Use knowledge of special-ist conventions to assist making, to introduce improvements and to explain what they are doing.	*Produce a report using models, illustrations, text and plans.*

10　• Use a range of techniques, processes and resources with confidence, safety and creativity to achieve high quality work.

Use a combination of computer-aided design and other high quality graphic techniques to produce a house style and image for a new company.

　• Review the design proposal during planning and making and show resourcefulness and adaptability in modifying the design in the light of constraints to make a high quality product.

Note: Pupils unable to communicate by speech, writing or drawing may use other means including the use of technology or symbols as alternatives.

The statutory orders in technology are set out in a different way from those in the core foundation subjects. The attainment targets are less about the content of the subject and more about the way of doing it. Educationists talk about the *process* of generating ideas, making and doing. The prime rationale for technology is the process approach, because it can extend over so many different subjects and contexts. Established subjects such as craft, design and technology (CDT), business studies, home economics and computer studies are all incorporated into this approach to technology. Other subjects, aspects of art and science for example, could also be included. A second difference in the statutory orders is that the programmes of study relate generally to the key stages for each profile component, rather than to each attainment target. This is to emphasize an integrated approach to the way the subject is taught.

The programmes of study are based around four key themes.

(1) Developing and using artefacts, systems and environments.
(2) Working with materials.
(3) Developing and communicating ideas.
(4) Satisfying needs and addressing opportunities.

To give an idea of what this means, an extract from the programme of study at key stage 1 is set out below.

PROGRAMME OF STUDY	EXAMPLES
Developing and using artefacts, systems and environments	

Pupils should be taught to:

• know that a system is made of related parts which are combined for a purpose;	*A bicycle; a house.*
• identify the jobs done by parts of a system;	*Bicycle chain; a kitchen.*
• give a sequence of instructions to produce a desired result;	*Prepare a shopping list in order of shops to be visited.*
• recognize, and make models of, simple structures around them;	*Making model buildings from simple construction kits.*
• use sources of energy to make things move;	*Stretched elastic bands to turn a propeller on a model plane; battery to make a toy move; moving things manually.*
• identify what should be done and ways in which work should be organized.	*Stamping a pattern on a fabric.*

Working with materials

Pupils should be taught to:

• explore and use a variety of materials to design and make things;	*Use a variety of materials such as cotton reels or building blocks to make a tower; making a collage.*
• recognize that materials are processed in order to change or control their properties;	*Yeast dough to bread; clay to pot.*

- recognize that many materials are available and have different characteristics which make them appropriate for different tasks;

  Fabric, paper, card, clay, paint, wood; clay for making a beaker; newspaper for covering the table when painting.

- join materials and components in simple ways;

  Gluing card, sewing on buttons.

- use materials and equipment safely.

At the secondary level the programme of study is in two parts. The first is for pupils working up to level 7, and the second is for those who will be studying at level 8 and beyond. Below are the two sections as they relate to the parts of the programme of study dealing with 'Developing and communicating ideas' and 'Satisfying needs and addressing opportunities'.

Developing and communicating ideas

Pupils should be taught to:

- analyse alternative solutions to produce a better design proposal;

  Consider alternative means for warning when a refrigerator door has been left open.

- design the appearance of an artefact, system or environment so that it appeals to users;

  Designing a radio for teenagers, furniture for adults.

- use modelling techniques to communicate design proposals;

  Prototypes, garment models, projection drawings, organization charts.

- use intuition as well as empirical data in developing their design.

Satisfying needs and addressing opportunities

Pupils should be taught to:

- develop a product and how to market, promote and sell it;

    designing and producing an entry system for a disco; a car alarm; a healthy snack food.

- investigate ways in which solutions could be extended to meet additional needs;

    Converting a wind-powered pump into a generator; adapt a fishing box for use as a seat.

- recognize the social, moral and environmental effects of technology;

    Considering the effects of a new motorway, intensive rearing, space shuttles.

- recognize and take into account in their designing that people can be an element in a system.

Developing and communicating ideas

Pupils should be taught to:

- present their proposals to an audience, using a range of methods and media;

- use computer-aided design, image generation and desk-top publishing to develop and communicate their ideas;

    Planning the detailed layout of a kitchen or recreation park; developing proposals for a company logo and letterhead.

- use symbols and conventions that have a meaning for an international audience;

    Designing working instructions, sign-posts for an airport; warning signs; using electronic symbols in printed circuit design.

- collate, sort, analyse, interpret and present information in a logical and coherent way;

    Justifying the choice of a site for a factory.

• recognize the place of experimentation and know that a new solution may be devised which has little basis in existing solutions.	*Linear induction motor; hovercraft.*

Satisfying needs and addressing opportunities

Pupils should be taught to:

• review the ways in which market research can be used to evaluate user requirements and market potential;	*Investigating the siting of a new supermarket; design of a graphics pen or drawing board.*
• understand that external influences (legal, environmental, social, health, safety) have effects on business activity;	*Considering the restrictions imposed by the Data Protection Act or the need for green belts around towns.*
• recognize the needs of individuals and groups from different back-grounds, when designing for their needs;	*The need for different food, clothing or shelter on the grounds of health, religion or culture.*
• recognize how economics affects design and technological activities and to work to a budget;	*Designing to a fixed budget; making aids for the elderly.*
• recognize the importance of the views of users and others affected by design proposals and take them into account in taking design decisions;	*High-rise and low-rise buildings; hypermarkets on the outskirts of towns; furniture design.*
• distinguish between objective and subjective criteria when evaluating.	

Some of the titles and phrases have a ring of unfamiliarity about them. 'Addressing opportunities' or 'Developing and using environments', for example, have only just come into the terminology of professional educationists, let alone the lay public. Technology, however, is a new subject and the way it is formulated for the National Curriculum is radically different from the myriad of versions of it that existed previously. A new subject needs new terms if it is to be meaningfully accurate across the variety of schools in England and Wales.

Most people are aware of the way this sort of change has affected information technology. Terminology that a few decades ago, if it existed at all, would have been familiar to only a few specialist scientists now features in dozens of magazines that can be found in newsagents everywhere. The statutory orders describing the programmes of study for information technology open with a number of general statements.

In each key stage pupils should develop information technology capabilities through a range of curriculum activities which will:

- develop confidence and satisfaction in the use of information technology;
- broaden pupils' understanding of the effects of the use of information technology;
- encourage the flexibility needed to take advantage of future developments in information technology;
- enable pupils to become familiar with the computer keyboard;
- encourage the development of perseverance;
- enable pupils to take greater responsibility for their own learning, and provide opportunities for them to decide when it is appropriate to use information technology in their work.

A detailed specification for the different key stages then follows. Given the widespread interest in information technology, both the programme of study and the attainment targets in this area are given here in full. These illustrate the sort of development and progression the National Curriculum aims to promote across the whole age range.

Programme of study for key stage 1

Levels 1 to 3 (ages 5 to 7)

Pupils should be taught:

- that control is integral in many everyday products, *such as cookers, cars, telephones*;

- that information technology can be used to help plan and organize ideas in written and graphical form;

- how to give instructions to electronic devices, *such as programmable toys and computers*;

- how to store, select and analyse information using software, *for example using a simple database package*;

- that information technology can be used for tasks which can often also be accomplished by other means.

In addition pupils working towards level 1 should be taught to:

- know that information can be held in a variety of forms, *for example words, numbers, pictures, sounds*;

- know that it is not always necessary to use the computer keyboard in order to produce information, *for example, by using an overlay keyboard to select musical phrases; by using a two-position switch to select from a menu*;

- control everyday items, *such as central heating thermostats and televisions,* and describe the effects of their actions.

Pupils working towards level 2 should be taught to:

- know that IT can be used to store, modify and retrieve information in words, pictures and sounds;

- organize and present ideas using IT, *for example using a simple word processor package.*

Pupils working towards level 3 should be taught to:

- use software packages confidently and well;

- locate information stored in a database; retrieve information and add to it; check the accuracy of entries.

Programme of study for key stage 2

Levels 2 to 5 (ages 7 to 11)

Pupils should be taught to:

- organize, develop and present ideas in a variety of forms by using software packages, *for example using a word processor or desk-top publishing program*;

- put existing information into a new format, *for example a newspaper, 'teletext' screen, message to a remote receiver,* taking account of the audience;

- use information technology to organize ideas in written, pictorial, symbolic and aural forms;

- work together to prepare and present stored information using information technology;

- know that programmable devices, *such as programmable toys and computers* can be controlled using sequences of instructions;

- use information technology for investigations requiring the analysis of data, *for example using a simple database*;

- know that information technology can be used to do things which can also be done in other ways, *for example using a database rather than a card index*;

- know that computers are used to store personal information, *for example medical records and commercial mailing lists.*

In addition for pupils working towards levels 2 and 3, teachers should refer to the relevant material in the programmes of study for key stage 1.

Pupils working towards level 4 should be taught to:

- find and present stored information, *for example retrieve text and amend it using a word processing program; retrieve an image and amend it, replay a musical composition and improve it*;

- insert and amend information in a computer database; test their procedures by checking how reasonable the results are, *for example comparing collected data with national statistics*;

- analyse the patterns and relationships in a computer model to establish how its rules operate; change the rules and predict the effect, *for example considering the way an adventure program responds to the choices made by the user*;

- review their use of information technology and consider applications in the outside world, *for example compare production techniques of a class newspaper with those of a commercial newspaper publisher.*

Pupils working towards level 5 should be taught to:

- collect and organize information for entry into a database, *for example design, trial and refine a questionnaire intended to collect information for a database*;

- know that the order in which instructions are presented, and the form in which they are given to a computer is important, *for example investigate the effect on a computer-controlled model of changing the order of the instructions*;

- write a simple computer program for a particular purpose, *for example a turtle graphics program to draw a street of houses; a set of instructions to operate a simple database program.*

Programme of study for key stage 3
Levels 3 to 7 (ages 11 to 14)

Pupils should be taught to:

- integrate more than one form of information, *for example words and pictures; symbols; pictures and sound*, into a single presentation or report for a particular audience;
  - *desk-top publishing to write about population growth, illustrating with graphs and charts; develop a sequence of screens of information to introduce visitors to the school, co-ordinated with a spoken commentary on a tape recorder;*

- work together to prepare and present information using information technology;

- use information technology to work more effectively;
  - *use a word processor for developing ideas for an essay; use a graphics program to investigate colour combinations for a design (instead of producing a series of design examples by hand);*

- know that each software item has its own strengths and weaknesses, and that the selection of software involves consideration of the facilities offered, ease and simplicity of use, availability and cost;

- select software for a task or application;
  - *choose between a word processing or desk-top publishing package to produce a book for young readers; choose between a database or spreadsheet program to store data about the additives contained in popular foods;*

- know that the use of information technology does not
  always provide an appropriate solution to a need, and that
  the effectiveness, appropriateness, and cost of alternative
  solutions must be considered;
  - *compare books, directories and databases as means of
    storing and presenting information;*

- know that information technology is used to monitor
  physical events and conditions, and to process, present and
  respond to collected data, *for example monitor the damp-
  ness of the soil around house plants, with a view to developing a self-watering system;*

- review and discuss their use of information technology
  applications and to consider related applications in the
  outside world, and their impact on daily life, *for example
  compare the setting up and running of a school viewdata
  system with that of a travel agent.*

In addition for pupils working towards level 3, teachers should
refer to relevant material for key stage 1.

In addition for pupils working towards levels 4 and 5, teachers
should refer to key stage 2.

Pupils working towards level 6 should be taught to:

- identify clearly the requirements, and make correct use of
  information technology equipment, software and techniques, in making presentations and reports;
  - *combining text and images in different ways for a news-
    paper report and a poster; composing and playing music to
    a class;*

- modify the data and rules of a computer model;
  - *examine the development of a simulated colony of pond
    algae by varying the rules of reproduction.*

Pupils working towards level 7 should be taught to:

- know that outcomes are affected by incorrect data,
  inappropriate procedures, limitations in the methods of
  data capture and the techniques of enquiry used to retrieve
  information; *for example compare the quality and quantity of
  data obtained by direct recording such as local weather
  statistics and remote recording by satellite monitoring;*

- translate an enquiry expressed in ordinary language into
  forms required by information retrieval systems;

- use search methods to obtain accurate and relevant information from a database; *for example use a database where knowledge of Boolean logic will improve the efficiency of the enquiry;*

- design a computer model for a specific purpose.

Programme of study for key stage 4

Levels 4 to 10 (ages 14 to 16)

Pupils should be taught to:

- work together, using discussion, explanation and negotiation, to improve the quality of the information presented using information technology;

- use information technology to improve efficiency and to support new ways of working;
  - *make use of a word processor for the entire development and production of a piece of written work; use information technology as a single means of accessing large databases instead of using a variety of printed sources of information;*

- select software appropriate for a particular task or application;
  - *choose between a word processing or desk-top publishing package, to develop a book for young readers; choose a database package which can handle large quantities of data, to set up a system to contain the results of a questionnaire for the whole school; choose an integrated software package to include the statistics from a database enquiry in a report;*

- know that there is an increasing range of methods of collecting data for computer processing, including many in which data is collected automatically, without human intervention; *for example bar-coded food and book labels; bank cash cards; computerized car park passes; medical monitoring systems;*

- design and implement an information technology-based system for use by others, *for example design a computer-based system for recording pupil choices and preferences of school meals;*

- review and discuss their use of information technology and consider applications in the outside world, and the impact on daily life, including environmental, ethical, moral and social issues; *for example word processors being more widely available in schools or offices; widely available portable telephones.*

In addition for pupils working towards levels 4 and 5, teachers should refer to key stage 2.

In addition for pupils working towards levels 6 and 7, teachers should refer to key stage 3.

Pupils working towards level 8 should be taught to:

- define the information required, the purposes for which it is needed, and how it will be analysed; and to take these into account in designing ways of collecting and organizing the information when creating a database, *for example create a database to enable a paint manufacturer to identify customers' preferences for colour and type of paint*;

- use information handling software to capture, store, retrieve, analyse and present information.

Pupils working towards level 9 should be taught to:

- evaluate methods of searching and sorting data manually and using a computer;

- know that the mathematical basis of a computer representation of a situation determines how accurately the model reflects reality; *for example a program to trace the trajectory of a tennis ball; a spreadsheet to anticipate trends in predator/prey populations*;

- analyse a situation, and then design, implement, assess and refine a complex model to represent it.

Pupils working towards level 10 should be taught to:

- analyse systems to be modelled using information technology, make choices in designing, implementing and testing them, and justify the methods they have used.

Attainment target 5: Information technology capability

LEVEL	STATEMENTS OF ATTAINMENT	EXAMPLES
	Pupils should be able to:	
1	• Work with a computer.	*Use an overlay keyboard to select items on a computer screen.*

- Talk about ways in which equipment, such as toys and domestic appliances, responds to signals or commands.

  Press a button to ring a door bell; turn a knob to adjust the volume of a tape recorder; observe the automatic switch on an electric kettle.

2
- Use computer-generated pictures, symbols, words or phrases to communicate meaning.

  Select furniture for a house displayed on the computer screen, using an overlay keyboard; construct a simple story as a sequence of words, pictures or sounds, using an overlay keyboard or mouse.

- Use information technology for the storage and retrieval of information.

  Write about 'today's weather' using a word processor so that the writing can be retrieved later.

3
- Use information technology to make, amend and present information.

  Use a word processor to draft a class diary; use information technology, with voices or conventional instruments to make music and replay it.

- Give a sequence of direct instructions to control movement.

  Give instructions to another pupil playing the part of a robot; control the movement of a screen turtle, using turtle graphics.

- Collect information and enter it in a database (whose structure may have been prepared in advance), and to select and retrieve information from the database.

  Enter data recording the birds using the school bird table, check the data and retrieve it to compare the numbers and types of birds on different days.

- Describe their use of information technology and compare it with other methods.

  Write about the differences between using a programmable toy and giving instructions to another pupil; identify the differences between using pencil and paper and using information technology for handling information.

4
- Use information technology to retrieve, develop, organize and present work.

  Produce a class newsletter or a set of information screens to give parents information about the school.

- Develop a set of commands to control the movement of a screen image or robot; understand that a computer program or procedure is a set of instructions to be followed in a pre-determined sequence.

  Drive a robot round an obstacle course or maze; use turtle graphics to draw a house.

- Amend and add to information in an existing database, to check its plausibility and interrogate it.

  Store personal information (such as name, height, weight, age, sex, shoe size, hair colour, eye colour), check it is correctly stored and find the names of girls and boys with particular characteristics.

- Understand the need to question the accuracy of displayed information and that results produced by a computer may be affected by incorrect data entry.

  Correct a file of data about individuals in the class in which some data has deliberately been entered incorrectly.

- Use a computer model to detect patterns and relationships, and how the rules governing the model work.

  Use a program which simulates a trawler looking for fish, or an adventure program with a clearly defined objective.

- Review their experience of information technology and consider applications in everyday life.

  Investigate overlay keyboards used in fast-food shops.

5
- Use information technology to present information in different forms for specific purposes.

  Edit a newspaper for parents; work together to produce a book for younger pupils.

- Understand that a computer can control devices by a series of commands, and appreciate the need for precision in framing commands.

  Investigate control systems such as automatic doors and alarm systems; make a set of computer controlled traffic lights.

- Use a software package to create a computer database so that data can be captured, stored and retrieved.

  Use information from a survey of prices of goods in local shops and markets.

- Use information technology to explore patterns and relationships, and to form and test simple hypotheses.

  Using a simulation, explore how the populations of predator and prey species fluctuate, and suggest when a predator is most active.

- Understand that personal information may be held on computer, which is of interest to themselves and their families.

  Collect correspondence received by their families which has been addressed using computer databases and discuss data needed to produce it.

6
- Use information technology to combine and organize different forms of information for a presentation to an audience.

  Produce a report which involves use of different fonts and letter sizes, and illustrations.

- Understand that devices can be made to respond to data from sensors.

  Use a computer to draw a graph of the temperature of a liquid as it cools; write a procedure, using a software package, to provide a warning sound if a light beam is interrupted.

- Identify advantages and limitations of data-handling programs and graphics programs and recognize when these offer solutions to a problem of data handling.

  Use a desk-top publishing program to integrate text and images in the report of a scientific experiment; choose a data-handling program for processing the results of sports day.

- Investigate and assess the consequences of varying the data or the rules within a simple computer model.

  Define or change the way information is grouped into columns in a spreadsheet showing the nutritional values of types of meals; modify a turtle graphics procedure or its parameters to draw a variety of shapes and transform them.

- Review experiences of using information technology and consider other applications and their impact on everyday life.

  Compare own use of control devices with bar codes used for automatic stock control in supermarkets; compare own expression of information using IT with computer-produced bills or personalized mail and consider the implications of access to personal information.

7

- Select software and use it to produce reports which combine different forms of information to fulfil specific purposes for a variety of audiences.

  Produce a presentation suited to a specific audience, combining graphics and text.

- Design, use and construct a computer model of a situation or process and construct computer procedures involving variables.

  Model the queue of people waiting at a supermarket check-out and vary the service time, number of customers and number of check-outs.

- Understand that the results of experiments can be obtained over long or short periods or at a distance using data-logging equipment.

  Use information technology to measure the acceleration of a model car as it runs down a ramp; interpret data transmitted by a weather satellite.

- Select and interrogate a computer database to obtain information needed for a task.

  Make use of a large database about careers or courses, and refine techniques of enquiry to select relevant information.

- Know when it is appropriate to use a software package for a task rather than other means of information handling.

  Consider the usefulness of a computer-aided design package to investigate the ergonomics of kitchen design.

- Understand that dangerous or costly investigations, or those not easily measured can be simulated by information technology.

  Experiment with the operation of a simulated nuclear reactor.

8
- Design successful means of collecting information for computer processing.

  Design and refine a questionnaire for collecting complex data in a form suitable for analysis by computer; use monitoring and data-logging equipment to record environmental change.

- Select and use software to capture and store data, taking account of retrieval, ease of analysis and the types of presentation required.

  Select and use database or viewdata software to provide information about local amenities.

- Construct a device which responds to data from sensors; explain how they have made use of feedback when implementing a system incorporating monitoring and control.

  Use software to record movement patterns of small mammals, and produce graphs and tables for use in a presentation; develop a robot vehicle which follows a path marked on the ground.

- Use software to represent a situation or process with variables, and show the relationship between them.

  Model and investigate the growth of bacteria using a spreadsheet, use a graph-plotting program to find a curve which fits a set of experimental data.

- Understand why electronically stored personal information is potentially easier to misuse than that kept in conventional form.

  Consider cases of computer fraud and unauthorized access to computer files.

9
- Evaluate a software package or a complex computer model; analyse the situation for which it was developed; assess its efficiency, ease of implementation and appropriateness and suggest refinements.

  Evaluate a computer-assisted drafting program used in technology; a graphics package used in art; a desk-top publishing program used in English.

- Design, implement and document a system for others to use.

  Design a system to investigate production schedules and stockholding strategies for a company making and distributing fast foods.

- Understand the effects of inaccurate data in files of personal information.

  Research cases where the use of inaccurate data has caused inconvenience; investigate safeguards on access to personal data in computer systems.

10
- Decide how to model a system, and design, implement and test it; justify methods used and choices made.

  Develop a system for monitoring the performance of a central heating system in order to plan a system for a house or school; develop a system for notifying parents that their child's immunization is due.

- Discuss the environmental, ethical, moral and social issues raised by information technology.

  Visit organizations making extensive use of information technology; prepare for the visit by deciding issues to be discussed with employees, such as how information technology was introduced, its effects on their work, their view of information technology; make suggestions about how the

*introduction of information
technology might have been
improved.*

Note: Pupils unable to communicate by speech, writing or drawing
may use other means including the use of technology or symbols as
alternatives.

The statements of attainment for technology have been quoted
in some detail. As a school subject, many aspects of it will be
unfamiliar to most people. The remaining six subjects (history,
geography, modern languages, art, music and physical education) are all compulsory in the National Curriculum and statutory orders are already or will shortly be in place to define what
schools should teach*. The statutory orders for the core foundation subjects and for technology have taken account of new
approaches to teaching and learning in each subject. This is
equally true in the other foundation subjects. The details of
programmes of study, attainment targets and statements of
attainment can be found in the statutory orders where
published. The chart below lists two or three developments in
the teaching of each subject that might distinguish the new
approach from that experienced by many adults when they were
at school.

History
- Emphasis is now placed on the skills of historical enquiry
  as well as the content of the subject. Distinguishing
  between alternative sources of evidence and making a
  judgement about their validity and reliability is one
  example. Pupils will be looking at primary sources such as
  original documents and letters in studying historical
  themes. This is particularly important in local history.

- Pupils are encouraged to explore alternative points of view
  and interpretations in looking at historical evidence.

- Twentieth-century and contemporary world and European
  history are now significant components of the history
  syllabus.

Geography
- The geographical context of social and political events
  (national and international) now features in the curriculum.

---

* *The publication of working party reports and final statutory orders receive widespread news
coverage. Many (English and history, for example) attracted considerable controversy.*

- The structure of worldwide economic interdependence is explored through a variety of geographical themes.
- Ecological and environmental issues are now included in the syllabus.

Modern languages

- Attempts are being made to make a wide range of languages (especially European languages other than French) available.
- Syllabuses now stress the importance of 'communicative' approaches to the teaching of the subject – less emphasis is given to strict grammatical accuracy. The key issue is whether the pupil is able to communicate in the chosen language.
- There is increased emphasis on oral and aural work in the modern language curriculum and in the associated tests and assessments.

Art

- A wider range of materials is now used in the teaching of art (textiles and batik, for example).
- In secondary schools links are now frequently made with other creative subjects (dance, drama, music) in formulating a coherent arts curriculum.
- The social and economic context and purpose of design are now included in many arts syllabuses.

Music

- Contemporary popular music in all its variations is now part of the music curriculum.
- Importance is attached to practical music-making as well as achieving understanding of musical notation.
- Individuals are encouraged to develop skills on a chosen instrument.

Physical education

- Teaching about health and fitness is now a significant part of the PE curriculum.
- Individual as well as team games are now encouraged.
- Links are being established with the creative subjects of the curriculum; dance, for example, features in many PE programmes.

SECTION 7

Special needs and
the National Curriculum

Many people are now aware that the school provision for children with special needs underwent revolutionary changes in the 1980s. The impetus came from a report on the education of handicapped children and young people published in 1978 (The Warnock Report). This established clearly that educational goals should be the same for all young people, regardless of any disability they might have. In 1981 an Education Act was passed, and in the following decade children with special educational needs who had been educated separately were gradually integrated into mainstream schools. A few special schools still exist, but for a very small minority of children.

The 1978 Warnock Report and the 1981 Act reflected the change in social attitudes to disability that has characterized the latter part of the twentieth century. Segregation in special schools had done little for the progress or self-esteem of many children, nor did it help promote sensitive, informed and caring understanding on the part of children or adults without disability.

Children who experience particular difficulties are likely to be the subject of what is termed a statement. With the agreement and involvement of parents, this will be drawn up by a group of professionals from a variety of backgrounds (educational psychologists, doctors, social workers and teachers). When the statement is complete, the school may receive extra resources to support the child's education. In drawing up the statement, careful consideration will be given to the extent to which the child can follow the National Curriculum. The NCC (National Curriculum Council) has made it very clear that children with special needs should have maximum access to all aspects of the National Curriculum. Only when this is clearly impossible will the requirements be waived (the rather unfriendly technical term *disapplication* is used in the legislation to describe this process). Whatever the outcome, the curriculum programme for each child will need to be broad, balanced and rich in opportunity for a full range of activities.

There will also be pupils in schools who are not the subject of a statement but who still have special educational needs. They also will need support. These children include those who follow the full National Curriculum programme of their peers but require specialist help with reading or numbers, and those who have been temporarily withdrawn from all or parts of the National Curriculum. This latter situation will only occur in a few circumstances – for example:

- where pupils have arrived from such a different educational system that they require a period of adjustment to the National Curriculum;
- where pupils have had spells in hospital, been educated at home or been excluded from school and need time to adjust;
- where pupils have temporary severe emotional problems (perhaps because of a family crisis) and need special arrangements.

The headteacher, with the agreement of the governors, has the power to make what is called a temporary 'general direction' to waive part of the National Curriculum. This cannot be done for longer than six months. The school is still responsible for the child's curriculum *and* it must ensure that a broad and balanced range of activities is offered.

All schools have now developed policies for teaching and supporting children with special needs. School prospectuses and governors' statements about the curriculum will almost certainly include a reference to the approach adopted. In recent years there has been a marked shift not only towards teaching special needs children in mainstream schools, but also towards teaching them in ordinary classes. Teachers with particular responsibilities for special needs children are therefore more likely to be working alongside their colleagues, giving group and individual support, rather than in their own specialist room or department.

Teachers, governors and parents should consider carefully the sorts of issues that inform the development of a special needs policy for the curriculum. NCC has produced guidance to help with this. In one document, *A Curriculum For All*, a number of questions are asked, for which the Council says schools should be developing responses. Examples include:

- Can the tasks and activities for any one attainment level be chosen and presented to enable children with a wide range of attainments to experience success? For

instance, emphasis on oral rather than written work
will help some pupils with learning difficulties.

- Can activities be matched to pupils' differing paces and
styles of learning, interests, capabilities and previous
experience; can time and order of priority be allocated
accordingly?
- Can the activities be broken down into a series of small
and achievable steps for pupils who have marked
learning difficulties?
- Will the activities stretch pupils of whom too little may
have been expected in the past? These pupils are likely
to include some with physical, sensory or other
impairment who are high attainers.
- Can a range of communication methods be used with
pupils with language difficulties?
- Will the purpose of the activities and the means of
achieving them be understood and welcomed by pupils
with learning difficulties?

The school environment plays an important role in developing
the learning of all pupils, but it is especially important for children with special needs. The layout of the classroom, the
capacity to change the way pupils are grouped, the provision of
information technology and other resources, and the encouragement of co-operative approaches to learning amongst pupils
can all support the integration of children with special needs
into the curriculum, and stimulate their capacity to learn.

The advice from NCC gives numerous ideas and examples of
how subject teaching in the National Curriculum can be sensitive to children with special needs. For example:

USE OF LANGUAGE

'Without water human beings are unable to survive' could
become 'People need water to live',

PRACTICAL ACTIVITIES

Pupils may be given paper for folding into a windmill shape.
Those with learning difficulties might need to have the
shape printed on the sheet with the folds marked. For a
visually impaired pupil the lines can be indented in the
paper with pressure from a ball pen or a spur wheel available from the Royal National Institute for the Blind (RNIB).
This creates an embossed shape on the reverse side of the
paper which they can feel. Even with extra help like this,

pupils will still need close guidance by the class teacher and classroom helpers.

CLASSROOM METHOD

Teachers will need to find ways to help those pupils who have specific learning difficulties in reading and writing to make use of their oral strengths (for example, use of tape recorder and word processor) and to ensure that evaluation and feedback on work are not over-dominated by hand-written products.

It is important that everyone involved is fully aware of the statutory responsibilities and regulations in formulating and developing policies. For example, the statutory orders for key stage 1 in English allow pupils to be exempted from attainment target 5, 'Handwriting', if they need to use a non-sighted form of writing or if they have such a degree of physical disability that the attainment target is impossible. This has implications for the way in which National Curriculum achievements are assessed and reported to parents. The Schools Examination and Assessment Council (SEAC), like the NCC, gives specific advice on how the regulations should be interpreted. Local Education Authorities also have officers and advisers who monitor the way the National Curriculum is taught in schools and can give individual advice to parents and teachers of children with special educational needs.

Parents, governors and the National Curriculum

Parents

One of the main purposes of the 1988 Education Reform Act was to provide parents with a wider choice of schools. Whether this has been achieved, or indeed whether it is desirable, is the cause of much debate. One consequence of the Act, however, is the existence of numerous statutory requirements to make available to parents information about the school's and their own child's curriculum. Some of these requirements were introduced in earlier Education Acts, in 1981 and 1986.

If you want to find out as much as possible about a school curriculum, you should:

1 Obtain copies of the statutory orders for each of the subjects – these are contained in loose-leaf folders. Every school* must have these available for parents to look through, and they can also be purchased through HMSO (see 'Further reading').

2 Look through the Local Education Authority's statement of curricular aims. These are available in schools and Local Education Authority offices – most main public libraries would also contain a copy.

3 Ask for a copy of the school prospectus which should contain the governors' statement of curriculum aims for the school.

4 Look through the school prospectus for the following information which must be included:

• a summary of the content and organization of that part of the curriculum relating to sex education (where it is offered);
• the hours spent on teaching during the normal school week, including religious education, but excluding the statutory daily act of collective worship, registration and breaks (including lunch);

---

* The regulations described in this section refer to LEA maintained schools.

- the dates of school terms and half-terms for the next school year;
- a summary for each year group, indicating the content of the school curriculum and how it is organized, including in particular how National Curriculum subjects and religious education are organized, what other subjects and cross-curricular themes are included in the curriculum for all pupils, what optional subjects are available and how choices among them are constrained;
- a list of the external qualifications (certificates) offered by examining bodies in specific subjects, approved under section 5 of the Education Reform Act, for which courses of study are provided for pupils of compulsory school age;
- the names of the syllabuses associated with the qualifications. A list of the external qualifications (certificates) offered by examining bodies in specific subjects, and the names of the associated syllabuses, offered to those beyond compulsory school age;
- details of any careers education provided, and the arrangements made for work experience;
- information about how to make a complaint, according to arrangements established under section 23 of the Education Reform Act;
- how to see and, where appropriate, acquire the documents to be made available under the Regulations.

5 Attend the annual parents' meeting and read the annual report for parents prepared by the governors. This must include a statement of any changes made to the information contained in the school prospectus.

6 Ask to see any schemes of work currently used by teachers in the school, or any syllabuses followed, whether for public examinations or otherwise.

These six sources of information must be made available to parents under the new regulations. In addition, from September 1st 1990, any *entitled* person must have access to curricular records and any other educational records relating to a registered pupil and kept at the school. An entitled person is defined as a parent of a pupil under 16, both the parent and the pupil when the person is aged 16 or 17, and the pupil only when aged 18 or over. Access to the records must be provided within fifteen school days of the request being made, and there is a system for a written request for corrections if the records are considered to be inaccurate. Schools have had to keep these individual curricular records from September 1990. The records should indicate how each child is progressing in all areas of the National Curriculum, including the levels reached in the profile components of each subject where these exist.

So far the legal requirements have been described. Most, if not all schools will be making arrangements that go beyond this. For example:

- There may be special parents' evenings where the curriculum for a particular subject or one year group is described in detail.
- Schools may provide visiting 'days' or 'times' when parents can drop in and observe classes. Timetable structures often make this easier at primary than secondary school, although at the secondary level parents' evenings may include 'sample' lessons with parents as pupils!
- The child's individual class teacher or tutor may make arrangements for contact at times when parents have particular concerns or queries.
- Annual reports to parents may be linked to an individual interview with the class teacher or tutor. At secondary level, subject specialists may also be available to help interpret the reports.

A good school welcomes parental interest and enquiries. It is, of course, important to remember just how busy a good school is! To turn up without warning and demand to see all the documentation described in this section would be unreasonable. It is also important to remember the importance of establishing the best possible relationship with schools and teachers. Some parents (and even some governors) have been known to approach the school with an element of suspicion, perhaps giving the impression of trying to catch someone out.

Through the 1990s all schools will be working out the most appropriate ways of implementing the National Curriculum. Every teacher will have to participate in training courses. Primary teachers have had to initiate a particularly wide range of new approaches. Allowance should be made for this in looking at a school's arrangements. On the other hand, parents should not be too meek in seeking out information or in ensuring that their child is receiving the full range of curriculum opportunities to which they are entitled. If you really feel that the school is not fulfilling the letter of the law, then Section 23 of the Education Reform Act ensures that each LEA establishes arrangements for considering complaints from parents. Every school prospectus, as has been shown, must contain information about how a complaint can be made.

Beyond all this, parents are now encouraged to take an interest in their child's progress through the curriculum. If, from the earliest age, children are made to feel that the different school subjects and topics are of intrinsic interest, this will have great advantages for their later experience of schooling. Model-making kits, books, atlases and colourful magazines all help with this. Some special National Curriculum packs are now appearing on the market. It would be wrong to be critical of all these, but you should remember two things:

- The National Curriculum should not become an examination; books that are really only an 'exam crib' should be avoided.
- The National Curriculum should not become burdensome to the child; this would be a severe blow to motivation and probably attainment. Any work at home should grow naturally from the school curriculum, and not be a means of forcing or pushing the child further than they need be at a particular stage.

Governors

Many of the concerns of parents and governors overlap. Governors have a particular responsibility to be responsive to the needs and interests of parents. They also have legal responsibilities for implementing the National Curriculum, and these must be clear to anyone taking the role of governor.

Every school has a governing body. The size varies with the size of the school, but it is always made up of a combination of parents, teachers, LEA appointees and co-opted governors. Headteachers have the choice of becoming governor, and the vast majority choose to join the governing board with full voting rights. All governors are appointed for a four year term.

Under their curriculum responsibilities, governors must:

- Ensure that the National Curriculum is implemented within the total school curriculum. They are also responsible for ensuring that provision of religious education meets the requirements of the law.
- Prepare a school statement of policy, bearing in mind the LEA's curriculum statement policy and ensuring, of course, that all the requirements of the National Curriculum are met.

- Determine the length of the school day and teaching sessions, within the data set by LEAs for terms and half-terms.
- Receive complaints from parents about the way the National Curriculum is working. If governors fail to satisfy the parent then the LEA agreed arrangements for complaints may be brought into operation.
- Agree and determine school financial expenditure, much of which will be linked to the implementation of the National Curriculum.
- Hold an annual meeting to which a written report of the work of the school and the activities of the governors must be presented – the report must be distributed at least two weeks prior to the meeting. Examination, and where appropriate National Curriculum assessment results must be included in the report.
- Submit annually to the LEA information about the educational provision they are making for pupils, including where the National Curriculum has been modified for certain pupils.
- Submit information about curriculum modifications for pupils who are the subject of a statement (see Section 7).

In carrying out their duties, governors will work closely with the headteacher and other teachers. The statement of curriculum policy, for example, may be drawn up following discussion of a draft prepared by the headteacher and other members of staff and by reference to the curriculum policy of the local Education Authority. The annual return of information about the curriculum will almost certainly be drawn up by teaching staff. If a pupil, perhaps through illness or because of behaviour difficulties, has to have the National Curriculum modified for a period of time, the governors will be advised by the headteacher. Governors do have significant responsibilities for the curriculum, however, and they will need to become conversant with the terminology of the particular approach adopted by the school. Most schools now arrange for governors to spend time in classes. At secondary level, particular governors may take an interest in different parts of the curriculum, although they should also be aware of the strategies adopted for whole curriculum planning. Governors have an important role to play in making sure that curriculum arrangements are described clearly to parents. Technical and obscure professional terminology should be avoided. To fulfil these responsibilities, Governors need to have more than a cursory understanding of the issues involved.

Implementing the National Curriculum

The National Curriculum will be implemented in stages throughout the 1990s. The chart on page 104 shows the dates when the different subjects must be taught at each of the key stages, and when children will receive national assessments that must be reported to parents. It is important to remember that each set of subject statutory orders is laid before Parliament after a complex consultation process. It is possible, therefore, that through the decade the chart will be modified. The assessment dates given here are likely to be changed. It is also important to remember that whether statutory orders are in place or not, schools should still provide a broad and balanced curriculum in key stages 1–3 and possibly key stage 4, covering all the subjects of the National Curriculum.

			KS1	KS2	KS3	KS4
mathematics and science	Introduced	Autumn	1989	1990	1989	1992
	First assessed	Summer	1991	1994	1992	1994
English	Introduced	Autumn	1989	1990	1990	1992
	First assessed	Summer	1991	1994	1993	1994
technology	Introduced	Autumn	1990	1990	1990	1993
	First assessed	Summer	1992	1994	1993	1995
history and geography	Introduced	Autumn	1991	1991	1991	1994
	First assessed	Summer	1993	1995	1994	1996
modern foreign language	Introduced	Autumn			1992	1995
	First assessed	Summer			1995	1997
art, music and physical education	Introduced	Autumn	1992	1992	1992	1995
	First assessed	Summer	1994	1996	1995	1997

Controversial and unresolved issues

This guide seeks to describe and explain the National Curriculum. Inevitably, given the scope and scale of the changes, there are now many publications critical of the structure of the National Curriculum, the way it has been set up and the approaches adopted in particular subject areas. Some of the sources of such literature are listed in 'Further reading' (see page 107). In this section, therefore, no attempt will be made to do justice to the wide-ranging debates that greeted the introduction of the National Curriculum and which, as in any democratic society, are likely to be sustained as long as central legislation exists. Instead, we will briefly list ten controversial and unresolved issues that governors, parents and teachers may become involved with at the school level.

Resources

Many teachers argue that insufficient attention has been paid to the resources needed for the National Curriculum. The statutory orders in some instances involve the wholesale revision of textbooks. Schools find it difficult to restock across a whole subject. There are also the costs of new equipment for subjects such as technology, and especially for information technology. The science programme involves primary schools in ongoing consumable supplies that were not previously required. Finally there is the issue of staff training and whether the money conceded by the government is sufficient to meet these needs.

Teacher shortages and skills

Now that every school has to provide a National Curriculum, the problems of providing appropriately qualified teachers are clearly revealed. Finding sufficient numbers of science, technology or modern language teachers is proving difficult in many parts of the country. There are shortages in other subjects such as mathematics and even English. In many years insufficient numbers of people come forward to train in these areas, and the difficulties therefore cannot be resolved quickly. There are also some shortages that are important, but less easy to observe. Some teachers of subjects such as English and mathematics have no qualification in the subject. It will be important to ensure that they receive adequate additional training, support and guidance. Similarly, in primary schools where teachers have to teach across the range of the National Curriculum, it is highly unlikely that any teacher will have sufficient grasp of all the subjects. Training and help is needed (and primary teachers rarely have the 'non contact' time usually allocated to secondary school teachers). It will be a challenge to provide the necessary support without too much disruption to existing classes.

Fitting everything in

There is a danger that the National Curriculum is becoming too dominant. It is now a major part of all schools' work. However, all the official documents make clear that there should be other aspects to the school's curriculum. In primary schools children should be allowed to pursue individual interests, follow up projects and so on. This is equally true at secondary level where it will be important to ensure a healthy take up of a second foreign language and subjects such as drama and dance. The detailed and prescriptive way in which the National Curriculum is set out may require so much attention that other things become neglected. This is particularly true at key stage 4, when the National Curriculum must be harmonized with the GCSE system. In January 1990 the Secretary of State, John McGregor, made a speech that focused on this area. He indicated that, in order to allow for the teaching of subjects outside the National Curriculum, pupils might be allowed to drop some foundation subjects early, provided they had reached level 8 across the attainment targets.

Some subjects seem to have been moved out of the National Curriculum

One of the criticisms of the National Curriculum is that the subjects are rather old-fashioned. Apart from technology, the list could have come out of a 1950s grammar school (or even one of the new secondary schools in the early 1900s!). Although you do not *have* to teach the National Curriculum in subjects, it is having a strong influence on the way people think and the way the curriculum is planned. Many people point particularly to the way in which art and music are stipulated, rather than the more broadly-based approach (adopted by most primary and an increasing number of secondary schools) of creative arts generally. In other words, are the arts going to become the low status part of the National Curriculum? Home economics teachers are also concerned about the status and importance of their subject if it is subsumed within technology.

Planning across the curriculum

Many of the areas left out of the National Curriculum, for example environmental education, economic awareness and citizenship, must now be taught with and across the programmes of study and attainment targets of the subjects. These topics involve highly significant issues for the last decade of the twentieth century. How are schools ensuring that they are covered? Are they really seen to be important by teachers, parents and pupils?

Recording achievement

In Sections 2 and 4 the question of achievement was discussed at some length. There is evidence that in some schools children's ability to achieve at the different levels is being prejudged. In other words, they are being typecast unfairly as unable to attempt more challenging and difficult work. The National Curriculum should always be used in a positive way to show what can be achieved next, never as a way of explaining what is impossible for certain groups of pupils. Equally, if the school only reports on National Curriculum achievements, then something will have been missed. There ought to be ways of acknowledging and recording the whole range of personal achievements.

Giving parents information

As Section 8 described, parents now have the right to a range of information about the curriculum and their child's progress. This ought to be seen as a minimum requirement, and not as the full extent of the obligation. In good schools parents are given information about a wide variety of curriculum plans and activities. They are also shown how their help and encouragement can ensure children progress with confidence and security.

Equal opportunities issues

There is now considerable evidence to show that certain groups of pupils are disadvantaged within the school curriculum. Research evidence suggests, for example, that girls are often disadvantaged by the design of tests and examinations. Children with certain special needs do not always receive the support they should. Race is also an issue in which inequalities have been extensively researched. Schools are expected to monitor the curriculum and assessment results and try to remedy any difficulties that arise. How this is done, however, is controversial and open to a variety of different approaches.

Over prescription of content and assessment

Many who have argued the case for a National Curriculum are unhappy about the highly prescriptive nature of the statutory orders. They also point to the inconsistent way in which the attainment targets have been formulated from one subject to another. The assessment system is seen as both detailed and cumbersome, occupying far too much of the teacher's time. In some countries a National Curriculum is prescribed which only covers 50 per cent of the child's time in school, leaving opportunities for local initiatives and a wider range of optional subjects and choices. Teachers are also given much more responsibility for making formal assessments without reference to bureaucratic, external regulations. It is possible, as the National Curriculum becomes fully implemented, that these issues will become an increasing cause of concern.

Dated content

England and Wales now have some of the most detailed curriculum requirements in the world. Knowledge in many areas, particularly in science and technology, evolves rapidly. Taking another perspective, some people have argued that many parts of the statutory curriculum (for example in history) are culturally biased and need modification. Will it be possible to revise the statutory orders sufficiently quickly to keep them up to date and responsive to changing social attitudes and values?

Further reading

Information about the National Curriculum can become dated very quickly. It is important, therefore, in looking for the statutory requirements, to purchase the relevant folders, such as *Science in the National Curriculum* or *Mathematics in the National Curriculum* (there is one for each of the subjects). They can be ordered through booksellers or direct from

HMSO
PO Box 276, London SW8 5DT

Each of the national councils also has an information section, producing a variety of helpful literature, including some specialist leaflets for parents and employers. The addresses are:

National Curriculum Council
Albion Wharf, 25 Skeldergate, York YO1 2XL.

Curriculum Council for Wales
Suite 2, Castle Buildings, Womanby Street, Cardiff CF1 9SX.

Schools Examinations and Assessment Council
Newcombe House, 45 Notting Hill Gate, London W11 3JB.

Additionally, the Department of Education and Science and the Welsh Office publish regulations and advisory documents:

DES, Elizabeth House
39 York Road, London SE1 7PH.

Welsh Office
Cathays Park, Cardiff CF1 3NQ.

A number of books have now been published that provide the historical and political origins of the national curriculum. Two authors – Denis Lawton and Clyde Chitty – have together and separately produced three interesting, critical volumes.

Chitty, C. (1987) *Towards a new Education System: The Victory of the New Right?* Falmer Press.

Lawton, D. & Chitty, C. (1988) *The National Curriculum*, 'Bedford Way Series', Institute of Education, University of London.

Lawton, D. (1989) *Education, Culture and the National Curriculum*, Hodder & Stoughton.

The most authoritative account of the whole of the 1988 Education Reform Act, including the curriculum clauses, is in Stuart Maclure's *Education Re-formed*, Hodder and Stoughton.

The Open University is producing a number of courses focusing on National Curriculum issues. 'Curriculum and Learning', first presented in 1991, includes text, television films, audio-cassettes and readers, and includes a discussion of a number of aspects of the National Curriculum. One of the readers – *New Curriculum – National Curriculum*, ed. Bob Moon, Hodder & Stoughton – includes a number of critical analyses of the period leading up to the implementation of the new legislation.

A journal, *The Curriculum Journal* published three times a year by Routledge for the Curriculum Association, is a valuable source of comment and analysis.

Schools and local authority advisory services will also be able to provide advice on publications which report the latest legislative developments in the National Curriculum.

Sources and acknowledgements

All extracts from National Curriculum statutory orders, all details of attainment targets, statements of attainment and programmes of study, and all other extracts from HMSO publications appear by kind permission of the Controller of Her Majesty's Stationery Office.

All extracts from NCC documents appear by kind permission of the National Curriculum Council.

p.13	Average Mathematics Proficiency and Average Science Proficiency graphs, from 1989 Report by the Center for the Assessment of Educational Progress in the U.S.A.
p.22	Extract and table from *A Framework for the Primary Curriculum*, published by the National Curriculum Council.
pp.29, 30, 33	Extracts from *A Guide to Teacher Assessment*, published by the Secondary Examinations and Assessment Council (SEAC).
p.37	Extract from *English Non-Statutory Guidance*, published by the National Curriculum Council.
p.37	Extract from *English for ages 5 to 11*, published by HMSO.
p.39	Newspaper extract from the *Oxford Mail*, 26 June 1987.
p.42	Newspaper extract from the *Sunday Times* magazine, 2 September 1973.
p.48	Extract on use of calculators in the classroom, from *Mathematics for ages 5 to 16*, published by HMSO.

114   *A Guide to the National Curriculum*

p.51   Examples of test questions, from *Mathematics for ages 5 to 16*, published by HMSO.

pp.57–60   'The contribution of Science to the school curriculum' from *Science for ages 5 to 16*, published by HMSO.

pp.61, 62   Science curriculum chart and approaches to primary science project, from *Science Non-Statutory Guidance*, published by HMSO.

p.66   Extract from *Technology 5–16 in the National Curriculum*, published by the National Curriculum Council.

pp.95–96, 96–97 Extracts from *A Curriculum For All – Special Educational Needs in the National Curriculum*, published by the National Curriculum Council.